FOLLOW
YOUR
HEART

FOLLOW YOUR HEART

A Foolproof Story of Success

By Philip Devitte and Erika Celeste

authorHOUSE®

AuthorHouse™
1663 Liberty Drive
Bloomington, IN 47403
www.authorhouse.com
Phone: 1-800-839-8640

Published by AuthorHouse   10/23/2012

ISBN: 978-1-4772-8451-3 (sc)
ISBN: 978-1-4772-8450-6 (e)

Library of Congress Control Number: 2012919895

CONTENTS

This book is dedicated to all who are in need of faith, willpower, determination, alignment, discipline, flexibility, and patience. Know that they are within you and always have been. And to the doctors, nurses, therapists, and counselors who helped me find myself again, even when we didn't see eye to eye.

This memoir is especially dedicated to my loving parents, sister Stephenie, brothers Rick and Curtis, and the rock and love of my life Ellen.

Thank you from the bottom of my heart.

PROLOGUE

Incense hung heavy in the air. Father Mark walked slowly down the center aisle swinging the thurible as blue wisps of smoke played about him, curling around his head and shoulders. Somewhere in the rafters church bells rang out long and low, signaling the beginning of the service. Rain fell on the slate roof punctuating the priest's every step with a soft ping, ping, calling the gray of the Seattle morning into the dark sanctuary.

A soprano joined with the rain in a mournful rendition of Ava Maria. First sweet and low, the melody grew in strength, ushering in an unending queue of parishioners.

Looking down at the little scene below me struck a chord deep within me. It touched my very soul to see how many family and friends had come: Mom, Dad, my older sister, Stephenie, younger brother, Rick, and their families; my childhood friend, Curtis, a few Eagles, people from the hospital, and many others I wasn't even sure I could name.

A lump rose in my throat when I spotted Ellen, my wife, in the front row. Her head was bowed, but there was no mistaking her fiery hair against the deep navy of her tailored suit. When she raised her head, the glint of tears sparkled in her eyes. I loved her with all my heart for being loyal to the end.

I'd put her through more than any one person deserved. We'd lived a hell beyond most people's worst nightmares, filled with enough pain and uncertainty to last many lifetimes. To truly appreciate the significance of my actions and their impact, we must turn the clock back to see how all of it and much more led me to where I was . . .

CHAPTER ONE

A LIFE-ALTERING MOMENT

I was excited to get back to the gang at work after a week off between Christmas and New Years. 1985 was going to be my year, I thought as I straightened my favorite red Italian tie. I had a gorgeous redhead for a wife, we'd just moved to the apartment of my dreams overlooking Lake Union in Seattle, and I'd just bought a BMW 320i. I'd always wanted a European car. This one had a sunroof and great stereo complete with graphic equalizer. The icing on the cake was that it was ice blue, my favorite color.

Jay hopped up on the counter and meowed in hopes of a treat, while I prepared a to-go mug of dark roast. Princess echoed her brother's request, winding between my legs.

"Not now, guys," I said, shooing them away with gentle pats. I brushed the cat fur from my charcoal gray, French suit, double-checked the contents of my briefcase, and headed for the elevator. I smiled to myself imagining the looks on everyone's faces when I made it to our insurance agency early, Dad's especially. He was a good boss, but rode me hard.

"Smile when you answer the phone," he'd remind me if I looked too serious during a call.

Shaking my head, I caught the reflection of myself in the elevator wall—just under six feet tall, built like a gymnast, light brown hair, and blue eyes. At a quick glance, the figure in the hazy metal might be mistaken for my father.

The floor bell dinged and I headed out to my new love. It was one of those sunny winter days that looked deceivingly warm despite being crisp and cold. But that didn't matter to me. In a town that was known for its rain, sunny meant one less day to worry about keeping my new baby clean and shiny.

Light traffic was already buzzing along the freeway. If I hurried I could beat the hustle and bustle of commuters, which inevitably turned the fast, flowing river of vehicles into a mucky, morning bog. The engine purred to life. I guided my BMW onto I-5.

There was a dusting of snow on the ground, but the roads were dry and clear. No one seemed too anxious to be getting back to work after the holidays, so we all zoomed along at a regular speed. I enjoyed my coffee and listened to the radio, patting myself on the back again for starting out early enough to make it in on time. *I could get use to this no rush stuff*, I thought lighting a cigarette. It was nice to take my time and do it right instead of scrambling and being stressed out when I arrived.

I switched lanes to prepare for my exit and hit black ice. Before I knew it, I was spinning hard and fast across four lanes of traffic. It was like an amusement park ride out of control. Cars were flying at me, yet somehow stayed out of my path as I wildly careened, then cartwheeled my BMW. The harder I tried to steer, the faster I spun.

Shit! I thought as I helplessly tumbled like a ragdoll. *There was no getting out of this one.* When I saw the car head for the shoulder I knew it would be over soon. I held onto the steering wheel for impact. *Whatever happens, happens.* All of a sudden there was nothing to be done and nothing to fear. I closed my eyes and went limp. Time and sound stood still. The next thing I remember I was flying through the air in slow motion. The whole thing was quite eerie like Alice in Wonderland going through the looking glass to another life, but it wasn't Alice. It was me.

Snow crunched beneath me as I dropped to the ground and rolled across a grassy knoll, chased by the metal scream of my sliding car. Then all was silent. *Holy shit,* I thought, closing my eyes, *I'm alive and there's not a scratch on me!*

I turned my head and saw my beautiful car in pieces less than a foot behind me and closed my eyes again. *She'd nearly crushed me. Talk about lucky!*

"Are you all right?" asked a female voice above me.

"Yes, I think so," I said looking into the face of a woman with short dark hair. I started to get up. "Hmm, that's strange I can't feel my legs."

"Honey, everything's going to be all right, but you need to stay still," she said preventing me from sitting up.

"No, I'll be all right, I just have to walk it off."

She smiled. "I'm sure you will, but just to be safe lie back."

I looked at her uncertainly.

"Trust me, I'm a nurse. Help is on the way." She busied herself taking my pulse and fussing over me. A crowd of people gathered to help. A blanket appeared and covered me.

As the minutes ticked by I realized that not only couldn't I feel my legs, I couldn't feel anything below my waist. *It must be shock,* I thought, *or the fact that I've been lying out on this frozen ground for so long. I should start wearing a seatbelt.* Thoughts shot through my head at lightning speed. *I need to call the office and tell them I'll be late after all. Wait until my wife hears about this. Should I have taken another route to work? When are they going to let me sit up?*

A state trooper leaned over me. "Sir, can you tell me your name?"

"Phil, Philip Devitte."

He patted my shoulder. "It won't be long now. The ambulance is on its way. Do you have someone you'd like me to call?"

"Yes, in my briefcase there's a little black book. Call my wife, Ellen."

"We'll take it from here," said a paramedic pushing through the crowd. He squatted down next to me. "Do you hurt anywhere?"

"No, I'm just numb. I can't feel my legs."

He gave a knowing look to his partner, who immediately radioed the hospital. While one contacted the emergency room, the other administered an IV.

"Do we really have to do this?" I asked. The ground was really cold and I just wanted to sit up. I had visions of going to my mom's for some of her chicken soup, a well-known family cure-all. I'd probably take a few extra days off. Be stiff and lay on the couch. Back to work by Monday.

But no such luck. The paramedics insisted I lay back on the stretcher while they loaded me into the ambulance. Within minutes we were headed to Valley General, sirens blaring and all.

Ellen's going to get a big kick out of this, I thought as we drove. I'd gotten into a million scrapes as a kid and always came out on top. I'd always been one of those people who assumed I could do anything. So as a four year old, it never even occurred to me that I didn't know how to drive. One day I decided to take the car for a spin, climbed in, put it in gear, and rolled out of the driveway onto the busy street. I caused quite a traffic jam and backed up a bus line. My mother was less than pleased when she'd grabbed the keys and removed me and our car from the street.

Stories like that and others had prompted the family saying, "That's just Phil." This was no different. It was just another Phil story to add to my long collection of adventures.

Someone touched my head lightly, and I opened my eyes.

"It's all right buddy, hang in there," said one of the paramedics.

It seemed like a really strange thing to say. I was fully conscious. I wasn't in pain. But he just kept giving me a look that made me wonder if he knew something I didn't.

Everything's going to be okay. This is all just a bunch of craziness. You're not going to die. It's all going to be over soon. You're going to go to the hospital and then Ellen's going to come pick you up.

The ambulance came to a screeching halt outside the emergency room. I watched the IV bag swing above my head and realized my back was starting to ache a little. The ambulance doors swung open, sending icy

5

air in to greet me. *Just in time,* I thought. *I'm going to need some pain meds when the shock wears off. Man, this is really going to hurt in the morning.*

A chill rippled through my body as they transferred me to a metal gurney and wheeled me in.

"Cut his pants off," directed a nurse as soon as I was in the ER.

"Whoa, this is a French suit," I said pushing the scissors away.

"The doctor needs to examine you," she explained as if that justified cutting into the expensive fabric.

"Then I'll hop out of them," I said starting to rise on my elbows

"No," she said holding me down. "It's important that you stay still or you could do more damage."

"Fine, but cut along the seams," I instructed.

She rolled her eyes but obliged.

A second nurse brought a pair of shears close to my neck. "Hold still, we have to get your tie too."

"Absolutely not," I said pushing her away. The suit was bad enough, but they weren't ruining my favorite tie. "Either untie it or I'm keeping it on."

The second nurse looked back to the first, then at me. "The more we move you, the more damage we risk."

I stifled a laugh. Now they were just being plain ridiculous. "I'll untie it myself, if you're afraid to."

"No." The nurse quickly undid my tie, folded it and placed it somewhere out of sight.

The throbbing in my back was growing worse by the second, but before I could ask for painkillers, I was wheeled off for tests and x-rays.

The minutes passed in a blur. Every time I opened my eyes, I was in a different room. Some were dark, others light, but I was always being poked or prodded. Strangely, I don't remember feeling much of it.

When I was very young, I remember going to get a shot. I must have squirmed for the nurse, because I distinctly remember her saying, "If you keep it up, I'm going to stick you again."

Years later when I told my mother about it, she refused to believe it. "I wouldn't have let anyone talk to you like that."

But I don't remember her being there, and I know what I know. I believe it contributed to a very real fear of needles. Just seeing one would make me light-headed. Yet, the way my back, neck, and shoulders were feeling quickly helped me overcome that fear. If there was even a moment's peace in a needle, I was willing to risk it. Tears streamed out of my eyes as I tried to catch the attention of a passing nurse.

"Please help me," I croaked. "My back . . ."

"I'm sorry, but I can't give you anything until the doctor examines you. It will only be a minute. Try to relax," she said, drawing a warmed blanket up around me.

Relax? Relax? I thought. *How can I relax when I can't feel my legs? Come on legs, please move. This had to be a nightmare.* But try as I might, I couldn't wake up.

I knew something had to be pretty screwed up for me not to feel my legs. But as much pain and agony as I was in, it never occurred to me what that thing might be.

"Sounds like you've had quite the morning," said a man in a white coat with glasses and blond, curly hair.

"Could I have something for the pain?" I whispered.

He smiled and scribbled on my chart. "I've sent a nurse to get something. I'm Dr. Cancro. Can you move your toe for me?"

I tried, but couldn't feel my either of my feet.

"Good," he nodded. "I'm going to stick you with a pin. Tell me when you feel it."

I strained to see what he was doing, but couldn't from my flat position.

"Okay, good."

I hadn't even realized he was touching me yet.

He flicked on an x-ray lamp in the corner of the room. "Can you see this all right?"

"Yes," I said, watching him put up a couple x-rays.

"The spine is broken up into several sections known as the cervical, thoracic, lumbar, and sacral curves. When any one of these is damaged it causes problems for the rest of the body, which may prevent it from moving properly. You have what we call a T-8 injury, or damage to your eighth thoracic bone in your vertebrae. Right about here." He pointed to a spot on the x-ray and then turned and pointed it out on his own upper back.

I nodded, fighting back the mind-numbing pain.

"You also have damage to your sixth and seventh thoracic vertebra. I can't see your spinal cord unless I cut open the bones surrounding it, which would of course do more damage. So we can't see the severity of your spinal injury. However, because of the way your backbone broke and how it stretched, I'm afraid I have some very bad news. It looks like you're paralyzed from the waist down."

"For how long?" I asked, not comprehending the magnitude of his words.

"For the rest of your life."

I shook my head. "No, that's not going to happen. I'm only 27 years old. I'm going to walk again."

"Phil, I wish I could tell you something different, but the reality is I've seen many injuries like this. Less than one percent ever walk again. The way your spine broke assures me of your prognosis."

"Well then, I'll just have to be that one percent."

Dr. Cancro gave me a sad little smile. "The sooner you accept it, the sooner you can move past it, and onto a full life."

"No, never," I said, tears swelling in my eyes as much from my back pain as from his words.

He sighed. "It's a lot to take in. Look, here's Suzy to give you something for the pain. You just need some time to rest and adjust."

I was so distracted by his words that I don't know if I didn't or couldn't feel the needle. Physical relief came quickly, but my mental anguish grew. *So this is what it's like to be paralyzed. I always thought being paralyzed was for the other guy. Something that tragic couldn't happen to me. I didn't deserve it.*

I couldn't and I wouldn't let that person be me. But then a little voice in my head said, *But it is you.* I was living the life of a paralyzed person. There was no deep dark secret as to how it had happened. It wasn't because I'd done something to deserve it. It was just one of those things that could happen to anybody. This time that anybody had turned out to be me.

CHAPTER TWO

UNENDING SORROW

The bad news didn't stop with being paralyzed. In a matter of moments, Dr. Yang, a neurosurgeon was by my side echoing the Dr. Cancro's ominous prediction and adding his own gloomy recommendations to the mix.

"We're going to have to stabilize your back to prevent further damage." He said the words as if he were attending a funeral.

I couldn't believe what I was hearing. Just moments before, I'd been a normal guy in the prime of his life. Now this joker was telling me not only that I'd never walk, but that things could get even worse. I couldn't picture what that might be and I certainly didn't want to find out.

Dr. Yang said something about several options and that he'd have to study my x-rays further before surgery to determine my best option, but I really wasn't listening. The mixture of painkillers and my new fate had my head spinning. I kept thinking, *This has got to be a dream. This can't be happening to me.* No matter how many times I heard it, it didn't sink in.

I'd never thought of being permanently disabled. Dying young, yes, but not disabled. I'd just always had this notion that there was some magic that exempted me from tragedy. Being crippled was not an option. The thought of spending my life in a wheelchair was

11

more than I could bear. I swallowed hard. *What a waste if this is all I'm going to be,* I thought bitterly. *How could you do this to me, God? Why me?*

Tears welled in my eyes as I thought about the future — no more basketball, no more hiking, no more driving fast cars. I'd never have sex, let alone children. Not to mention I'd be stuck in Depends for the rest of my life.

"There you are!" Ellen rushed into the room and hugged me.

I winced as the pressure of her embrace lulled me from my drug-induced state. But I dared not move for fear of Dr. Yang's warning. "Hi," I croaked.

"We were so worried about you," my mother said, patting my legs.

It was the strangest sensation to know I was being touched and yet feel nothing. If I hadn't been looking her direction, I wouldn't have known it at all.

"I've had better days," I said giving her a weak smile. "Have you talked to the doctors?"

Ellen and my mother exchanged glances. "Yes."

"Then you heard? They say I'll never walk." My voice cracked as I voiced the words that wouldn't stop echoing in my head.

Ellen grabbed my hand and squeezed.

"They're wrong. I'm going to walk again. I know I can do it."

"Yes you will. I know it too," said Ellen, tightening her grip on me.

Mom looked away.

"Mom, it's all right. I'm going to walk again."

"Hey, there's my number one son," said Dad coming into the room, followed by my younger brother Rick, before Mom could reply.

"What'd I miss?" asked Rick trying to lighten the mood.

"Not much, my whole life just changed in a split second," I said. "You know me, just being Phil."

They all smiled at the spark of what was quickly becoming the old Phil.

"You know, the kicker was I was going to start the New Year off right. I was going to be on time for work this morning."

"So you had to find a way to get out of it?" joked Dad.

"You know me, anything for attention," I said, explaining what happened.

Dad furrowed his brow. "How are you really feeling?"

I sighed. "I'm okay." Then bit my lip, "But they say I'll never walk again." I looked directly into my dad's eyes and said in a voice much stronger than I felt, "I don't care what they say. I will walk!" My gaze bore into his daring him to defy me.

He nodded. "I know you will son. They're only doctors. They don't know everything."

Just hearing my dad say that made all the difference in the world. It was like being a little kid again, when he could cure my every cut, bruise, and bump with a hug and a few soothing words. Somehow knowing that Dad believed I could do it gave me the strength and reassurance I needed.

"Can we get you anything?" asked Rick.

"No, but could you let Curtis know?"

13

"Sure thing," he smiled.

Curtis had been my best friend since we were kids. Then I thought about all my other friends—especially the ones who'd elected me president of the Eagles.

"And can you let the Eagles know about the accident? Tell them that I can't make tonight's meeting, but I'll try to be at the next one in two weeks."

"I'll let the guys know," Ellen assured me.

"The office was so quiet without you last week," said Rick shaking his head. "I should have known you'd figure out a way to get more time off. We're going to miss you."

Dad clapped Rick on the back. "Don't worry about anything except getting well."

"All right everyone, I don't know where you're going, but you can't stay here," said a nurse, shooing my family out. "It's time to get cleaned up."

Ellen kissed me on the cheek. "I'll be right outside if you need me," she whispered before following the others out.

It wasn't until I was alone with the nurse that I realized I hadn't cleaned up yet. Besides my broken back, I had a huge gash in my left leg. It looked as if someone had scooped the flesh out of it. Dirt and dried blood covered my body, and my hair was full of glass and grime.

"For someone who's just been in a car accident, you certainly don't have many cuts or bruises," said the nurse cleaning my leg wound.

"Yeah, I guess not."

"Any idea how you got this doozy?" she asked dabbing at my leg.

"It all happened so quick. They say I went through my closed sunroof. I guess it happened then."

She sucked in a breath. "Sorry if this hurts."

"I wouldn't know," I said, still in awe of the fact that I couldn't feel a darn thing below my waist.

"Sorry," she said going pink. "I didn't realize . . ."

"That's all right. I'm only beginning to realize myself."

She finished bandaging me and left. Alone in the silence of my room, thoughts raced through my head like a freight train. Just this morning I had walked to my car like any other day, completely unaware of what was about to happen. There had been no warning at all, one minute I was fine, the next they were saying I was a cripple. It didn't make sense.

The more I tried to reason, the crazier the whole thing seemed. I thought back over the last few weeks before the accident and wondered if the universe had tried to warn me. Just before Christmas, I'd been sitting at my desk, waiting for a call, when I'd started doodling. I'd drawn tiny stick people. As I drew each little man I thought about how important it is to have a back. I erased one of the back lines and considered what that would mean to a real person. It occurred to me that breaking your back would be one of the most terrible things that could ever happen since your back is what basically holds up your whole body. Had I unintentionally wished something upon myself?

Just two nights ago, I'd celebrated New Years. I'd dressed like it was summer, wearing boat shoes and a light jacket even though it was cold out. I loved those shoes. They were so easy to kick off, and I reasoned once we got to the hotel – which was quickly becoming an end of the year tradition – I'd be so hot from partying that I'd be glad I'd dressed lightly.

After dinner my family and I walked back from the restaurant to the hotel. In the short while we'd been gone it seemed like the temperature had dropped 10 degrees. The cold pavement beneath the thin soles of my shoes turned my feet to ice. The light jacket just made matters worse. The Don Johnson look might fly in Florida, but it definitely wasn't working for late December in Washington. To fight the cold I would run and then stop and let Ellen catch up then I would run again and stop. By the time we reached the hotel my feet were in serious pain. I'd abused them like they were nothing. Now I couldn't even feel them. Had it all been some kind of karmic foreshadowing?

What was I going to do with my life now? I wondered, staring at the sound-absorbing tiles in the ceiling. My career had already been chosen. I was destined to take the reins of my family business. I had been right on track, happy with my life. I had everything and was exactly where I wanted to be. And yet something deep down inside me had been calling out, was I supposed to be doing something more than just selling insurance?

I closed my eyes. Not that any of it mattered now. It wasn't like I could aspire to greatness in this state. I longed to stretch or turn on my side, but dared not move for fear of Dr. Yang's words. My doctors' words played in my head like a broken record. *You'll never walk again, you'll never walk again, you'll never walk again.*

I didn't believe them. I couldn't. But somewhere deep inside me a little voice asked, *What if they're right? What if they know something you don't?*

But then something even deeper, a knowing beyond knowing told me it wasn't true. It wasn't denial, this was a deep knowing at the core level of my being. It was something I knew about myself just as much as the fact that my eyes were blue. I could hide them behind shades or colored contacts, that might lead people to believe they were something else or some other color, but I knew what they were and would never be convinced otherwise.

Later that day, my sister Stephenie and best friend Curtis came to check in on me, followed by several other friends and family. Seeing everyone parade by my bedside made me feel like I was witnessing my own funeral. Their solemn faces and guarded words made me want to pinch myself, just to make sure I was still alive.

Toward evening, Mom came by with Dr. Lavallee, one of my parents' best friends. He was a true blue Canadian and looked every bit the physiatrist that he was, complete with wavy unkempt hair, glasses, wool sweater, and a pipe. I'd known him since I was a kid. His family always joined ours for Dad's annual Christmas Eve beef stew, a reading of *A Christmas Carol,* and midnight mass.

I brightened when I saw him. He was a learned man who always gave good advice and really knew his stuff.

"How are you doing?" he asked with the same worried expression friends and family had been giving me all day.

"I'm all right," I said tired of the same conversation, yet again.

Follow Your Heart

"Your mother tells me the doctors have given you a pretty serious prognosis."

I nodded. "They say I'll never walk again—but they're wrong. I know I will."

"Do you understand how serious a T8 break is? It's not like a broken arm that heals in a few weeks. Less than 1 percent of these kinds of injuries ever walk again."

I hadn't expected this kind of talk from Dr. Lavallee. He was always at the head of the class when it came to pep talks and encouragement. "I know myself. I know what I'm capable of, and I know that once they give me a chance, I'll do it. I will walk again."

"Denial is the first stage of grief when we lose something important to us. The quicker you move past it, the quicker you can accept your fate and move on with your life."

"My fate? It hasn't even been 24 hours and the medical world is ready to write me off."

"We're not writing you off, but you really should listen to your doctors. You can't take what they say a la carte, believing some things and rejecting others. You must be reasonable. What you're expecting is the impossible. It would take a miracle. They just don't happen that often, that's why they're miracles."

"If that's what you need to call it, that's what I'll have."

"The longer you fight the adjustment, the more difficult it will be. I'm afraid you're setting yourself up for a very big disappointment. It's difficult enough to recover from such severe injuries. You don't need to fight the depression that comes from disappointment too."

"Thank you for your concern, but I'm really going to be just fine."

"A lot of things are about to change in your life, and you're going to need to be reasonable and stay mentally strong to adapt."

"I'm not going to adapt to anything. I know what I can do and have a family and wife who believe in me. That's all I need."

"That's another thing. Ellen's a young, active woman, there may come a time when she can't handle this . . . she may not want or be capable of spending the rest of her life with someone in your shape."

"Ellen's not going anywhere," I said firmly.

"She may want children, and you can't fault her for that."

"She's not going anywhere." I ground out each word slowly and distinctly.

"Look, all I'm saying is that people change. You're going to have to give her some space, be flexible, and understanding if the time should come . . ."

"I think you need to leave."

"Refusing to talk to me won't change your circumstance."

I shifted my gaze to my mother. "Please see Dr. Lavallee out."

"Denial only makes things worse," he said again as he rose to leave. "Please keep an open mind and think about what I've said. I only have your best interest at heart."

"Goodbye, Dr. Lavallee," I said wishing more than ever that I could roll over and turn my back to him.

"Dr. Lavallee, what a pleasant surprise," said Ellen, coming into my room.

"He was just leaving," I said coldly.

She watched him leave with my mother. "What was all that about?" she asked when they were out of earshot.

"He wants me to accept my fate as a cripple, and he says you're going to leave me."

"What?" she asked, furrowing her brow. "Where'd he get that information?"

I shook my head. "He says that's what people often do, when circumstances change."

"Well I'm not going anywhere," she said, eyes blazing.

I looked away feeling the tears welling. "I would understand if you did." I swallowed hard. "This isn't what you signed up for."

"This isn't what you signed up for either," she said coming around the bed to look me in the eyes. "It just happened. And if you recall those vows we took, we didn't say 'for better only,' we said, 'for better or for worse.' I don't know about you, but intend to live by them. So honey, you're stuck with me until death do us part."

"You say that now, but you have no idea what you're getting yourself into."

"I'm strong. I can take it."

"You shouldn't have to take anything."

"And neither should you. But who says life's easy?"

"I'm wearing a damn diaper!"

"Then I guess I'll learn to change it, you big baby," she said putting her hands on her hips.

The look on her face was so determined I couldn't help but laugh. It was all so absurd I just couldn't help myself. She started to laugh too, then bent over me and kissed my forehead.

"As long as we have each other we're going to be just fine. Our marriage is our business and no one else's. That was extremely rude of Dr. Lavallee to say about me. He doesn't know what's going on in my head. I'm not some statistic that easily gives up on her husband, just like you're not some statistic that doctors can place a number on and predict your future. Who cares what their data shows? They're not gods. We have the free will to prove them wrong."

Ellen stayed until late in the evening. Neither of us wanted to spend the night apart. I could count the number of times we'd slept separately since we'd been married. We'd come so very close to losing each other that morning. Though neither of us said it, we knew the other was thinking it.

That night after she'd gone, I lay in bed thinking about her. I loved her so very much. She was everything I'd always wanted in a mate — beautiful, smart, kind. Talk about fiery and tough—she had it all. I met her on a blind date. Even though I was casually seeing someone else, my friends said I had to meet her.

We agreed to meet at a Seattle bar with our friends. She had her red hair up in French braids, which I didn't think much of, but I loved her big blue eyes. It was October, and after a few drinks we thought it would be fun to go to a haunted house.

I dropped her off at her apartment so she could change while I waited in the car. When she came down, va va voom! She took my breath away. She'd taken her hair down, so that it flowed and swung loose around her shoulders. And her jeans, boy did she know how to fill them out! She had more curves than a racetrack.

On the way to the haunted house, I learned she was a country girl, which just added to her mystique. Being from the city, I'd always wanted to date a country girl. When we went in the haunted house, she got scared and grabbed my arm. For the rest of the tour she held on to me really tight, and that sealed the deal. From that day on, I'd never wanted anyone else.

Ellen's words, after those of Dr. Lavallee, touched to my very core. My heart beat with pride when I thought about the depth of her loyalty. I wondered if she would always stay that way, or if she'd get sick of me. Dr. Lavallee might not be right about my walking, but his words about Ellen really bothered me. She was active and young. She deserved someone who could do all the things she could do. I knew she wanted children. She deserved children. Now I might never be able to give them to her . . . and sex. I loved sex. Nothing might be working below my waist, but I was still a guy. Just seeing her turned me on. I didn't know if I could go a lifetime without sex. How could ask her to do the same? Thoughts of Ellen and our life together spun in my head until, exhausted, I fell into a deep sleep.

CHAPTER THREE

NO ESCAPE

Sleep was my only bliss in those first few days. At least when I was dreaming I didn't feel pain, could still walk, and was in control of my life. It was a whole other story when I was awake. I couldn't turn myself, dress myself, or feed myself. There was someone to take my blood, another to poke and prod for vital signs, and yet another to give my medicine. I was completely at the mercy of others, including pain control.

Sometimes I believed the doctors when they told me I'd never walk. I'd tried and tried to feel my legs, but how was I supposed to do something that had always come automatically? Moving was instinctual. No one had ever shown me how to do it. As far as I knew, I naturally tried as a toddler and eventually succeeded. And the physical feel of movement – that sensation we get when we decide to take action – happens automatically. We don't stop to consider putting a foot in front of the other to walk, stepping up to ascend a staircase, or using our legs to brace against a fall. We know what it feels like when it happens, but we don't know exactly how that process works. Unless you're an expert in ambulatory science or some related field, you don't even know the words to describe that process or those sensations. It just is.

Without that information, I had no clue as to how I would make my legs work again. I hated the idea of never walking again. At these times uncertainty would cloud my foggy brain. That little voice in my head would convince me that the doctors were right and only doing their job.

But at other times, the idea that the doctors knew more about my body than I did really pissed me off. They'd given up on me without ever trying. That, in itself, made my blood boil. How could they know what I was capable of? They didn't know anything about me. At times it seemed their only mission was to shut me down. They said it was for my own good. That the sooner I accepted my fate the better off I'd be. That living in false hope was more damaging to my emotional state than losing my legs.

Easy for them to say, I smirked to myself in a brief moment of lucidity. *It's easy to take it all in stride when it's not you. I wonder how willing they'd be if someone said the same things to them that they're saying to me?*

More often than not, I would thankfully pass out after such thoughts. Visitors passed by my bed in a whirlwind of names and faces. Beneath heavy lids, I tried to focus on them and what they were saying. Sometimes it was hard to remember if I'd actually seen them or if I'd just dreamed they were there. Those who couldn't come in person often called to check up on me. It was a welcome distraction from the constant pain, which would come on quickly once the drugs started to wear off, a problem since I was on a timed regimen. And so my life swung in a pendulum of drug-induced stupors and pain-wracked lucidity.

Flowers, cards, and gifts came from everywhere. Many of my Eagle brothers and sisters sent mementos from round the state. It seemed like there were several deliveries a day. I was overwhelmed with the outpouring of love and compassion. It reminded me of the last scene in the movie *It's a Wonderful Life* when George's friends and family stop by to make sure he's okay. I only hoped I'd have as positive an outcome as he did.

A few mornings after I'd arrived, Dr. Cancro stopped by on his usual morning rounds.

"Have you experienced any movement?" he asked pulling back the covers without waiting for a reply. "You know the routine, let me know if you feel any of this." He pulled a needle from his pocket and tested my legs and feet.

I inhaled and held as still as possible in hopes of feeling the slightest pressure. But the truth was, with my eyes closed I'd never even know he was touching my feet.

"What about this?" he asked moving my foot back and forth.

"No," I mumbled.

"Or this?" He bent my leg slightly.

"Maybe we need to try a different treatment. What about an experimental drug or something?"

He straightened his glasses and came around to the head of the bed. "Phil, you need to understand something. The longer you go without movement, the less likely that you will regain function."

"But there has to be a cure."

"No," he shook his head. "There isn't."

"But I know I will walk again. I dream about it every night. I can feel it deep inside me. We just have to put our heads together to figure out what it is."

"I'm sorry, that's not going to happen."

"How can you say that? You've never even given me a chance!"

"I know because this is what I do. I've seen plenty of T-8s. They just don't recover."

My blood pressure began to rise. His audacity was unreal. He wasn't even referring to me as a person, now I was just a T-8. "Bet me," I said before I realized the words had escaped my mouth.

"What did you just say?"

"You heard me. Bet me. Bet me that I'll never walk again and I'll bet that I can."

"I'm sorry, I don't make bets with patients."

"Because you know you'd lose this one."

"Because I don't play with my patients' health. And because it's completely unrealistic to fuel your enthusiasm for the impossible."

The fact that he was so sure I'd never walk again became my motivation. He was so dismissive that I had to prove him wrong. Granted, I desperately wanted to walk for the betterment of my own life, but his complete denial fueled me with an even deeper passion. It was a challenge that I couldn't let go unanswered. The look on his face, when I strutted into his office one day would be the icing on my cake. I began to fantasize about that day, rehearsing different scenarios in my mind. Sometimes I'd confront him directly. Other times I'd bump into him on the street. But the end goal was always the same – the priceless look on his face when he realized how wrong he'd been. I'd just smile and say, "Never say never!"

Dr. Yang echoed Dr. Cancro's diagnosis, but admitted that I may gain some mobility back. He kept a close eye on my spine with daily visits. As the swelling went down in my back, he was better able to see my injuries and decide on a course of action.

"We're going to have to do surgery to stabilize your spine," he informed me a few days after my arrival.

I vaguely remembered him saying something like that, but quite frankly hadn't been sure if it was real or a dream. I tried to focus on his mouth so that I could better understand the words coming out of it. Shouldn't there be someone here with me? I wondered trying hard to think where Ellen was. He was using big words and rambling on. She'd know what he was saying. I tuned back in just in time to hear . . .

"I believe the best option will be to fuse your back."

My tongue felt thick as sandpaper. "Fuse it? But I need my back. Won't that mean I'll never be able to move?" A sharp pain coursed through my body and I cried out. "I think my medicine is wearing off."

He pulled my chart from the foot of my bed and then checked his watch. "You should be good for another hour.

"Please," I panted as pain spread through my upper torso, dripping white-hot pain.

"I'm sorry, we can't give you too much, or you risk addiction."

"I don't care. I need something."

He sighed. "The more we give you the more you'll need to stop the pain. We need to hold off for as long as possible."

All of a sudden my abdomen tightened with a jerk. Before I realized what was happening my legs snapped toward my chest.

"What's happening?" I asked in a strangled voice.

"Just try to relax," said the doctor massaging my legs and lowering them back into place. "Breath nice and slow, in and out."

I tried to follow his directions, but he seemed to be talking to me through a very long tunnel.

In, out, in, out, I breathed the way my mother had taught me when I was learning to meditate.

" . . . was a spasm," Dr. Yang was saying. "With spinal injuries, the less your legs are used, the more likely it is to happen. It's fairly common for what you're going through."

I closed my eyes and continued to breathe. "You said something about surgery?"

He hesitated. "Yes, as you know the back is made up of many tiny bones that all work together to bend. I plan to fuse a few of those bones together by using a piece of your hipbone."

"From my leg?" I asked, wondering if I'd heard right or was dreaming again.

"Yes, then I'll use some rods and wire to strengthen your spine."

I opened my eyes to stare at him. His lips kept moving, but the words they were saying didn't make a lot of sense. *Why did he need my leg to fix my back?*

He must have read my confusion. "Look," he explained sketching everything out on the back of my chart. "I'm taking this piece from your hip and putting it here. Then we'll strengthen it like this. You won't be able to move as much of your back as you used to, but you will still be able to move it."

"Maybe you should talk to Ellen," I said closing my eyes again. "Tell her why I need this."

"I'll speak with her tonight. But I want you to know that, given your injury and the level of recovery we might expect, this will be your best option. Without it, it's hard to say what might happen. But I can tell you that the risk of further damage will be much greater."

"Okay," I said inhaling deeply. "When do we do this?"

*   *   *

The following 48 hours passed in a drug-induced blur. Everything in my body – or at least the parts I could feel – ached with such ferocity, it was all I could do not to cry.

I had the continuous strange sensation that I was crossing my legs. I'd get excited thinking my feeling had returned only to look down and realize they weren't crossed and hadn't moved an inch.

On the day of my surgery, my good friend, Father Mark, came to see me. After exchanging friendly greetings, he got right down to business.

"Have you received Last Rites yet?"

"What?" I laughed. "That's only for dying people."

He frowned. "It's for anyone in a serious situation."

"Now you're scaring me. Has the big guy told you something I should know?"

"No, no nothing like that. Anointing of the sick is just a precaution to make sure any ill or injured person will go straight to heaven should anything happen."

"I don't know, it seems kind of silly to me. I've lived through the worst part. Maybe you should have

29

been there to give me rites before I got in my car the other morning."

"Indeed I should have. But all the same, better safe than sorry."

"All right," I conceded. "Let's do it."

Father Mark heard my confession, anointed my forehead with oil, and gave me communion. A nurse came into the room just as he placed the Eucharist on my tongue. She bowed her head reverently for a moment while he finished. But as soon as "amen" left his lips, she was all business.

"Time to go, Mr. Devitte. The O.R. waits for no man."

She pulled the rails of my bed up, unhooked various monitors and my I.V., and lifted the brakes on the bed wheels. An entourage of nurses and orderlies took up positions around the bed and pushed me into the hall followed by my family and Father Mark. The procession wound its way through a maze of corridors, onto an elevator, and down several floors.

When we reached the operating room doors, my entourage parked my bed and disappeared. The nurse who had prepared me turned to my family.

"This is where you say your goodbyes."

My father squeezed my hand. "Things are about to get a lot better for you. You'll be feeling fine in no time," he assured me.

I wasn't so certain. I'd always hated needles. When I was a kid, Mom told us one morning that she wanted Stephenie and me to be ready outside our school precisely at three because we had an appointment that afternoon.

"What kind of an appointment?" I asked.

"I'm taking your to get your vaccinations," she explained.

"You mean shots?" I squeaked.

All I could think of all that day was that big needle and how much it was going to hurt. I usually watched the clock with great anticipation, willing the minutes to go by faster, so that school would be over. But that day I prayed it would never end. I hoped Mom would forget. And I even considered dragging my feet, so that we'd be late and miss the appointment. But I knew better than to incur my mother's wrath. Instead, I formulated a much more brilliant plan.

When my mother arrived, I got in the car and calmly let her drive us to the doctor's office. As soon as the vehicle came to a stop, I sprung from the car with lightning quick speed. I ran blindly to the nearest tree and scaled it like a spider monkey.

"Philip Devitte, come down here immediately," Mom ordered.

But I refused to budge. There was no way I would ever leave the tree willingly. In fact, I could see myself living in it for an extended period of time if I had to. If monkeys in the jungle could do it, I didn't see why I couldn't.

Unfortunately, Stephenie had a better plan. She talked some older boys, who were passing by, into climbing up after me. I put up quite a fight, but between the three of them they were able to haul me down, more or less intact.

Needles, the sight of blood, and doctors in general had always given me the shivers. I'd always thought I would rather die than have surgery. In fact, I thought it was entirely possible that I was the biggest chicken in the world. If I had the ability to get up and run like I had when I was six, I would have. Then again, that was the reason I was there in the first place.

My mom leaned over and kissed me. "Don't worry, everything's going to be just fine."

Before I could protest, Ellen was by my side. "Has anyone ever told you how brave you are?"

I snorted. "Nice try. You know I'm scared shitless," I whispered.

"Yes, but you're doing it anyway," she whispered back.

"Like I have a choice."

She smiled. "I'll be waiting right here when you wake up." She planted a quick kiss on my cheek before my drill sergeant of a nurse wheeled me away.

The operating room was stark and bright. It reminded me of another planet with all the silver hoods hanging from the ceiling and medical personnel in masks and gowns.

"Hi Phil," a man near my head greeted me. "I'm Dr. Marturello. I'm going to be your anesthetist."

"Do you have any questions before we get started?"

"You should know, I'm terrified of needles," I blurted out.

He chuckled. "Don't worry, there are no needles here. I'm going to take good care of you. Now just relax and I'm going to put this mask over your face. I want you to take several deep breaths through your nose and count backwards with me . . . 100, 99, 98 . . ."

My breath sounded like Darth Vader as I slowly inhaled and exhaled . . . 97, 96, 95 . . . before I knew it I was out. I floated in peaceful darkness, unaware of my surroundings. I don't think I even dreamed.

The next thing I knew, I was coming-to. Slowly, a strange room came into focus. When I tried to move, it felt like a linebacker had mopped the floor with me and then thrown my lifeless body under a semi-truck.

Ellen's face appeared above me. "Welcome back," she smiled.

"Hi," I breathed groggily and promptly passed out again.

That night after everyone had gone home, I awoke all alone in the incandescent glow of my monitors. Tubes and wires covered me, pulsing to the beeps and hums of machines that looked as if they belonged in a sci-fi movie. As I began to focus, I remembered where I was. The nightmare that had become my life hit me like a ton of bricks. Fear mingled with panic and pain shot through my being until I didn't have a single pore that was unaffected.

The night nurse heard me stirring and gave me morphine to stop the pain. I'd never had it before and boy was it strong. It didn't take long before I was extremely sick to my stomach. Vomiting is never pleasant, but when you can't move it's downright scary. Beads of sweat lined my forehead and drool ran down my chin as I tried to regain control over the little bit of my body that I still could. Luckily, my stomach was empty from surgery, so I didn't have to worry about a lot coming up. Stomach acid burned the back of my throat and a bitter taste lingered in my mouth. But I was too exhausted to do anything about it and soon fell into a deep sleep.

Soon I was dreaming about Smurfs. The little, blue elf-like men marched around, as they sang their la-la song and happily worked. Then they saw me and went crazy. A whole gang of them grabbed me and beat me up. There were so many—like ants that I couldn't fight off. They tied me up, threw me in their van, and took off. Then Snoopy, as the Red Baron, appeared in his plane. He fought off the Smurfs and rescued me.

I woke up screaming and the nurse came running.

"Are you okay?" she asked.

I looked around the room panicked and feeling like I'd been beaten up. Then I remembered what had really happened.

"Do me a favor," I said breathlessly. "Please don't give me any more morphine. I can't handle the stuff."

The next day my friend Jay came to visit. "Hey buddy, I brought you something," he said, pulling a Red Baron Snoopy out from behind his back.

I smiled at the irony, but never told Jay about my nightmare. At least he hadn't brought me a Smurf. I named the stuffed animal Fire Dog and placed him above my bed like a talisman to guard against future nightmares.

Unfortunately, Fire Dog couldn't protect me from the worst pain of my life. The wounds from surgery hurt even more than the ones from the accident. I'd never been one for pain medication in general because I didn't have a strong stomach and hated the doped up side effects that went with them. In the past I'd foregone medication and just dealt with my temporary discomforts. But this was far different. It was a deep, white-hot throb that made me want to crawl out of my skin. There was no escaping it. From the moment I opened my eyes to the moment I passed out, it was my constant and unwelcome companion. Without morphine, the medical staff's arsenal of painkillers was severely limited. And like everything else, it was given on a timed schedule that left huge gaps between when it lost its potency and when I was allowed to have more.

It was all I could do to stay sane and felt like I was constantly asking for something to relieve my pain. But more often than not the nurses' responses were snide or unfeeling.

"I just gave you a shot."

"You need to be patient."

"You've had enough. You need to relax."

They made me feel like I was an addict or something. Quite frankly, I didn't care. Addict or not, I needed pain medication.

In addition to severe pain, I was now in a body jacket—a kind of molded plastic cast that resembled a turtle's shell. The thing was seriously uncomfortable. Not only was it hot and unventilated, but it made me feel claustrophobic. I've always had a fear of confined spaces. The body jacket made me feel as if I were in an iron lung. There was no real way to breathe deeply or expand my chest.

To make matters worse, there was nothing I could do about it, since I was unable to turn myself. Just days before, I'd been independent and free to do as I chose. Now I was confined. Caged like a rat. Between my claustrophobia and loss of independence I thought I would go crazy.

I comforted myself with the knowledge that I would be free of the torture device in a matter of hours. But the next morning, the doctor told me I would have to wear it day and night. He said I could only take it off to dry, after I had my shower. I would have to wear it for the next 5 months!

Then I remembered what my mother had been through. When I was about nine, she had to have back surgery. She'd been in a full plaster body cast for what seemed like forever. All she could do was lay in bed in a great deal of pain. When the cast finally came off, she discovered that the pain didn't go with it. Fed up with traditional medicine and the lack of results it had promised her, she set out on a quest to find something better.

It was the Age of Aquarius. Technically it meant that the planets, sun, moon, and Earth were all in the Aquarian constellation. But for many people in the sixties, it signaled the Golden Age of humanity and a time of peace. For Mom, it was a window into a world void of pain.

She got into yoga, found her chi, and eliminated most of her pain. She also got into astrology and explored eastern philosophy. Oms and incense became a way of life in our house.

"What is she doing?" I asked Stephenie the first time I saw Mom meditating. Mom was sitting in the lotus position, arms balanced on her knees, thumbs and forefingers forming circles.

"Shh, she's concentrating," cautioned my sister.

Mom opened her eyes, and patted the floor next to her. "Come sit."

We joined her, one on either side.

"You know how I haven't been feeling well?" she asked.

We nodded.

"Well this is kind of like recharging my batteries. When I do this everything in my body starts to work better."

As far as I could tell, she just looked like she was sitting on the ground singing to herself. I didn't see how that could help anything. I cocked my head. "How does it work?"

She smiled. "Make this sound: Ommmmm." She hummed until the mystical noise reverberated throughout her whole body. "Everything around us is made up of energy, the Earth, the trees, this floor, even you and me. We can use that energy to help or hurt ourselves and each other depending on how we use it."

"Kind of like super heroes?" I asked.

"Yes, in a way. Telling ourselves we like who we are, or that we can do something, sends our minds and bodies healing, positive vibrations or energy. Telling ourselves we're no good, lazy, or stupid not only makes us feel bad about ourselves, but it can even make us sick."

"So the vibrations help you feel better?" asked Stephenie.

"Not just me, anyone. The best part is you don't have to be hurt or sick to use it, we can do it at anytime."

Stephenie and I scrambled to sit like Mom. She adjusted our arms, helping us to form perfect finger circles. Then we all practiced our Oms.

Thinking back on that gave me newfound respect for Mom. Medicine had advanced so much since I was a kid. She must have been in massive pain, yet for the most part she carried on like it was no big deal.

I wished I could be more like her, but my body jacket severely added to my pain and discomfort. The only thing that seemed to help was being turned. It got to the point that I was asking to be flipped every 15 minutes—and even that took all I could do to wait.

When I buzzed the station again to ask for another flip, my nurse came in with a scowl. "Yes? What do you need?"

"Could you please turn me again?"

"I'm sorry, we have to limit your number of turns to every 30 minutes," she said briskly and started to walk out.

"But wait, you've been flipping me every 15 minutes."

"And we shouldn't have been. Do you know how much time and energy that takes? Turning is a two-person job and there are several patients on this wing that need our help. We can't devote all our time to just one person."

"Please, you can't imagine how uncomfortable I am. It's all I can do to control the pain."

"Mr. Devitte, you're not the only one on this floor in pain," she said strolling out of the room.

After that I could swear the nurses took their sweet time answering my call button. Hospital rules required them to do so, but it often seemed like an eternity until someone would show up. And if it was so much as a minute under my allotted 30-minute turns, they refused to help me.

Anger boiled inside me. How dare they make me feel like some kind of criminal for asking for relief. They had no idea what I was going through. "Try walking a mile in my shoes," I growled into my quiet room.

With no one to answer I vented into the silence. What did those dumb bitches know anyway? As far as I was concerned everyone could just go to hell. Screw the world! If God and the universe were so good, how could he let this happen to me? Had I done something wrong that I wasn't aware of? Was this payback for some misdeed?

Why me? Why me? Why me? I raged into the darkness. No one understood what I was going through. No one had any idea. My whole world had been ripped away from me like I was some pawn in a sick, twisted game.

Well if this is the way it's going to be, then I don't want to play, I thought bitterly. I just wanted to die. If there was a way to kill myself, I would have seriously considered it. But I couldn't move more than a few inches and those stupid nurses had everything that might come in handy for ending it all well out of reach.

CHAPTER FOUR

LIFE IN A CHAIR

I had high hopes that my legs would come back after my back surgery. It wasn't something I dared voice, it was more something I had just assumed would happen. As if having surgery was the magic pill to jumpstart my stalled life.

I didn't have to remain perfectly still now that my back was stabilized and I was wearing the body jacket. So I did exercise the ability to move my arms and head more freely, but that was about all I could move.

It seemed like every night I had dreams of playing basketball or walking on the beach with Ellen. My friends would marvel at how well I'd come back and congratulate me. We'd laugh at the wonderful turn of events and take off on our next adventure, hiking, skiing, or rock climbing. Then I'd wake up and expect to see my legs move. When they didn't, I'd get frustrated and angry.

I never got angry enough to give up on my goal of walking, but each day that passed with no change increased my doubts. A few days after surgery, the doctors moved ahead with their plan to have me accept my fate as a paraplegic.

"We're going to get you into some physical therapy, so you can start using a wheelchair," said Dr. Cancro after his usual morning examination, which had yielded no results.

"I'm still going to walk, you know." I knew that I had to use the chair to get my strength back, but it irked me like you wouldn't believe that he seemed to think plopping me in a wheelchair was the end goal.

"We've been over this Phil . . ."

"Yes, we have and I don't see why you have to set the bar so low. You're encouraging me to do the least instead of pushing for my best. Isn't there some kind of doctor's oath about helping patients recover to the best of their ability, not status quo or 'good enough'?"

"My job is to help you recover, not give false hope." He made a quick notation on my chart.

Even that really ground away at me, because I knew he was marking "no change" and dismissing me as some crazy patient who couldn't accept reality.

My physical therapist, Suzanne, arrived shortly after the doctor. After lying in bed for nearly two weeks and not eating much, I'd lost all my strength. My legs and arms had atrophied. It was strange to think how quickly I'd physically changed. Just a week before the accident, I'd bench pressed 170 pounds, now I was scrawny. Moving the dead weight of my body took every bit of strength I could muster. It felt as if I'd scaled Mount Everest by the time I pulled myself into a sitting position. With seconds my head started to spin and I felt incredibly dizzy.

"Whoa," she said helping me to keep my balance. "Being light-headed is very normal. Just wait a few minutes and it will pass."

I shook it to clear the cobwebs and took a couple deep breaths. "Okay ready."

"That's great," she said when she saw my determination. "Sitting up after so long is a great feat for your first day. In fact, most of my patients would be too tired to go on." Her eyes twinkled. "Do you need more time to rest?"

"No," I panted. "Bring it on. What's next?"

"Now you need to learn how to transfer yourself from your bed to a wheelchair."

I looked at the chair, which was about a foot from the bed. A few weeks before, I wouldn't even have thought twice about the distance. Now it looked like the Grand Canyon. "How am I supposed to get way over there?"

"Since you can't use your legs, you're going to use a body transfer board," she said, holding up a board about 2 feet in length and 6 inches across. "This creates a bridge from your bed to the chair." She laid the board down as she explained. "The goal is to slide yourself across it and onto the seat."

I slowly moved myself even with the board and scooted until I could drop one leg over the edge and then the other. I inhaled deeply, taking in a mixture of cleaning supplies and medicinal odors, the benchmark scent of hospitals. As I was transferring I got really scared of how high the bed was off the ground. It seemed miles from the floor. *What if the board slides out from under me and I drop?* I thought. *My legs can't help me.* I started to tremble. *Maybe I was in over my head.*

Suzanne was right there at my side. "Steady now, easy does it," she said as she helped me complete the transfer.

"Think I'm going to be sick," I said the moment my bottom hit the chair. My head was spinning like a merry-go-round. I was so dizzy I thought I would pass out.

"Just relax, take deep breaths," she instructed as she lowered the back of my chair to a 45 degree angle.

I lay there for several minutes with the world swimming around me. If I closed my eyes, I would almost believe I was on a boat. Slowly but surely the sensation wore off.

"I think we've done plenty for today," said Suzanne squatting beside my chair. "Let's get you back in bed."

Suzanne said I got sick because I sat up for such a long time without working up to it. "You've been lying down for so long, it's going to take a little bit for your equilibrium to readjust itself."

Over the next couple of days I continued to practice. By the third day I was able to transfer myself and sit upright in the wheelchair.

That was a big deal for me because it meant I was gaining some of my independence back. I could now make my way around the hospital on my own.

* * *

"If I could be like Mike," I said wistfully to Curtis as he wheeled me to the cafeteria. In my eyes Michael Jordan was the man to aspire to. He had fame, success, money—and I believed could have whatever his heart wanted or desired.

"Yes, we all know if only you'd grown another 6 inches, you could have been an NBA star," he said shaking his head.

I'd always had a habit of blaming my height for whatever trouble I was having at the moment.

"Okay, let's hear it. How would being like Mike get you out of your current situation?" he asked.

"Well if I was a basketball star, I wouldn't have been going to work at the insurance agency for one, so I would never have been on that highway."

"No, not good enough," said Curtis. "You'd still have to go to work at whatever arena you were playing in. The only difference is you might take a plane instead. And there's no rule that says Michael Jordan's plane can't crash. Instead of being injured, you might be dead."

"Well fine, then, maybe I just wish I was like that guy," I said nodding toward a patient who was standing by the nurses' station laughing with some of the women behind the counter.

"I'm not so sure you should say that. Maybe he's terminally ill or something."

"No," I shook my head. "He doesn't look ill. He has no idea how lucky he is. I see patients like him passing my door all the time, without a care in the world."

Curtis chuckled. "They must have some or they wouldn't be here."

I ignored him and continued. "I see them in my dreams. In no time the lucky S.O.B.s are released from the hospital. They laugh and joke all the way down to their cars because they know they can leave their wheelchairs behind once they hit those doors. They know that they'll have a full recovery and enjoy life."

"And you didn't have problems before the accident?" he asked, pulling my chair into the elevator.

I scowled and continued my rant as the floor lights lit up. "Not me, I'm the lucky sap who gets to transfer my body into the car and take the wheelchair home with me. Thank God I survived the crash!" My voice echoed off the walls of the small enclosure. "How merciful of him to spare me. Of all the things on the planet to happen to me, it had to be something that has no cure. How could I be so fortunate? Thank you, thank you for this wonderful and awesome gift."

"Okay man, that's enough, the elevator's going to open in a second and your family's looking forward to seeing you up and about."

"Yes, better put on a happy face for the family. God forbid I upset them," I grumbled as the bell rang and Curtis pushed me out into the corridor. A surge of panic overcame me as I realized this was my first time outside my room for anything other than medical procedures. It was almost like being back out in public.

My parents, brother, sister, and Ellen were waiting for us. When they saw me, they all clapped.

"Look at you," said Rick, "those are some pretty fancy wheels."

"That's my boy," said Mom kissing my cheek.

I smiled and tried to act casual, but my heart was beating a million times a minute. To my family, being in the cafeteria was a big step toward recovery and assuming a normal life. But I thought being in such a public place magnified my disability. I was certain everyone was staring at me.

I couldn't get to a table fast enough to hide the fact that I was in a wheelchair. The others followed suit and found their places before going up to order their food.

"What can I get you?" asked Ellen.

Eating itself was still a bit of a chore. My stomach had shrunk considerably since the accident and it didn't help that I'd had several bouts of nausea while learning to use the wheelchair. "I'll take something light, a salad if they have it."

She leaned down and hugged me. "You are looking so much better. I'm so glad you're coming back," she said before going to get my food.

I watched her leave and marveled at how strange it was to see people in something other than scrubs or hospital gowns. They all glided along with no cares in the world, unaware of what charmed lives they were leading.

One by one, my family returned to the table with their meals until we were all assembled like Thanksgiving Dinner. The only problem was I wasn't feeling particularly thankful. The more I looked around the cafeteria, the more I realized how out of place I was.

"Honey, your dad just asked you a question," said Ellen, nudging me.

"Hmm, what?" I asked, turning distractedly to him.

"I was just saying how proud of you I am," said Dad. "You've come a long way in such a short time. When did you start working with the wheelchair?"

I shifted uncomfortably. "Three days ago."

Everyone murmured their approval. But their doing so just made me more self-conscious. I could swear everyone in the cafeteria was staring at me. The fact that my family kept talking about my disability as if it was the most normal thing on earth just made it worse.

"I can't do this," I said to Curtis. "Could you please take me back to my room?"

"What? But you just got here," said Mom.

"Please," I said still looking at Curtis. "I really don't feel well."

"Have some food," suggested Dad. "You'll feel better once you have something in your stomach."

I looked around feeling more desperate by the moment. Why wouldn't anyone help me? I just wanted to go back to the safety of my room, where no one would stare at me.

I looked at Ellen for help. She'd always been able to read my thoughts.

But she just smiled. "Everyone came all the way over here to eat with you. Why don't you stay a few more minutes?"

"You guys just don't get it. You have no idea what this is like. You're all acting like it was some miracle I survived. But it wasn't. This is the cruelest trick God could play on anyone. I wish I was dead."

Ellen put a hand on my shoulder to try and calm me. But I shrugged it off. If people hadn't been looking at me before, they certainly were now.

"What kind of stupid idiot are you?" I asked her. "Why the hell would you want to be with a cripple like me? You must be pretty screwed up and have just about zero self esteem to stay with a guy who can't even have sex with you properly. Maybe I don't want you either. Did you ever think of that? Why don't you divorce me instead of acting like Mother Teresa? Who do you think you're fooling?"

"Okay, that's enough," said Curtis, getting up and pulling my chair away from the table.

Ellen's big blue eyes had filled with tears, but I didn't care. I wanted her to hurt and my family to hurt, the world to hurt as much as I did. It served them all right for walking around like it was no big deal. If I could cut their souls as deeply as mine had been cut, maybe they'd realize what I was going through.

Mom and Stephenie closed ranks around Ellen, while Rick helped Curtis take me back to my room.

"What's your problem?" asked Rick once we were in the elevator. "Ellen's been nothing but kind and you just treated her like a class A jerk."

"You guys don't know what it's like . . ."

"Yeah, yeah, we've heard it all before," he said coming around to face me in the small, space. "You act like you're the only one affected by this accident. Have you ever stopped to consider what this has done to the rest of us? How Mom's had bad dreams about you? How we have to pick up your work at the office? How your wife has to take care of your business and sleep alone at night? So pardon us for rallying around you and being supportive. Pardon us for trying to hold our family together. How could we be so selfish? It is after all just about you."

"It's not like that." I fired back aching for a fight. "I . . ." But my mouth quickly closed as I realized it was like that. I'd never thought about what my family had been through. Until Rick called me on it, I'd never really stopped to consider it from their point of view. Once I did, the air went out of my balloon. I was so busy being angry and taking it out on the world that I hadn't realized how much the accident had hurt my family.

We rode the rest of the way in silence. When the elevator opened, I half expected Rick to stay on it and return to the rest of the family. But he got off and followed our tight-lipped procession down the hall and into my room.

He helped Curtis silently lift me into bed. He was like our other brother. Our bond was so tight that the three of us were often able to work together without words. Mom's friend Lois said it was because we'd spent many lifetimes together as warriors.

Right now my warrior brothers didn't look too happy with me. I wasn't too thrilled with myself either. I couldn't believe what I'd just said to everyone, especially Ellen. I'd never spoken to her like that in my life. I wouldn't be surprised if she really did want to leave me now.

"I really acted like an ass back there," I said once I was situated in bed.

"You can say that again," said Curtis.

"I should go apologize to Ellen."

"No, I think you've done enough for one night," said Rick. "Give her a little space."

"I'm sorry guys, I was a pretty big jerk to all of you. Thanks for getting me out of there. Will you apologize to everyone for me?"

Curtis raised his hands and took a step back. "That's something you're going to have to do yourself."

"I was just so overwhelmed. I felt like everyone was staring at me and when no one wanted to help me back to my room I felt like a caged animal. I panicked and just had to get out of there."

"So you went after Ellen?" he asked.

I hung my head. "She was just closest and I was a ticking time bomb." I looked Curtis and then my brother in the eyes. "I just wanted you to know, I've never done anything like that before. I just hope I didn't ruin things between us."

If I thought I felt bad before, it was nothing in comparison to the way I felt when I realized how I'd hurt my family.

Curtis checked his watch. "Listen, I have a meeting and I left my coat downstairs."

I nodded. "Sorry again. I just got overwhelmed."

"No problem," he said clapping me on the shoulder. "I'll chalk it up to the drugs talking."

I smiled, but it didn't go all the way to my eyes. I'd really screwed up and all I could think about was fixing it.

"Looks like it's just us," said Rick plopping into the chair next to the bed. "That is if you promise not to bite my head off."

I nodded. We sat in silence for a few minutes lost in our own thoughts. Night had fallen on the hospital. Even though there weren't a lot of windows to tell me, it just somehow seemed darker. The lights would get brighter, and there was this general hush that amplified small sounds.

"I get so scared sometimes," I confessed to Rick. "What if I never get my legs back? What will my life be like then?"

Rick shook his head. "You can't let yourself think like that. You have to stay positive."

"But when you hurt as much as I do, that's much easier said than done."

"Yes, but think back to right after surgery. You hurt less than now than you did then, right?"

I nodded. "It's getting better."

He smiled. "So that's a positive. You're better now than you were a few days ago and you'll be a little better tomorrow."

"Yes, but this," I gestured to my wasted body, "is not what I want."

"There are a lot of things in life we don't want, but they happen and we have to deal with them. This one just happens to be a big one for you."

I shook my head. "Before, I had everything. I didn't have a care in the world."

"That's not true," said Rick. "You're idealizing the past. You had a good life before the accident, but you still had problems. You sometimes had an occasional client that mouthed off or you didn't much care for, you still had to pay taxes, you still got colds and the flu."

I shrugged. "Everyone has those problems. This is special. Not everyone ends up in a wheelchair."

"My point is your life wasn't perfect. No one's is. You still had some unpleasant things to deal with. Before the accident you would have thought those things were a pretty big deal. But everything is relative. It just depends on your perspective."

"Well, from this perspective, I've lost everything."

"No, you haven't. You've gained a lot."

"Are you crazy? What have I gained?"

"You can't judge yourself based on before the accident. That's a different person. He's not here now. I think you have to look at it from where you've come from since being injured. If you do that, you've made a lot of progress."

I snorted. "It doesn't feel like it. Remember that cartoon we use to watch, *Mr. Wizard*?"

"With the turtle that'd always beg to go to different times and places?"

"Yes, and then once he was there he'd always get in trouble and say, 'Mr. Wizard take me back home.' I wish I had a Mr. Wizard."

"You do. You have many Mr. Wizards, starting with yourself, then your family and friends, and even the hospital staff. The only difference is none of us can wave our wands to make things happen. It's going to take a lot of work."

"I suppose," I said, shifting in the bed. "Oh, does that hurt! Rick, could you rub my back?"

Rick came over. "Where does it hurt?"

"Right between my shoulder blades, no lower, okay a little to the right. Yes that's it."

"You always could get me to do anything. Remember the time you decided to give me a haircut?"

"Hey, I'd never given one before. I figured five was the perfect age to start."

"Mom didn't think so when she found all my hair on the floor with the clippers."

"You looked like a half-shaved monkey," I laughed.

"You're lucky you didn't cause some deep-seated childhood trauma." He continued to knead my back. "Who knows, there may still be something buried so deep it will take years of therapy to fix."

"Hey man, I made you stronger. It helped develop character."

"I doubt it. Convincing a three year old to try Dad's cigarettes is not character development."

I laughed. "To be fair, I just lit them up. You didn't even try to smoke yours. I had to do that all alone."

He chuckled until he snorted, which made me chortle.

"Oh, stop, it hurts!" I panted between laughs. But I was on a roll. I couldn't stop. It just all seemed so funny. I was in some crazy, stupid, mixed-up dream that I couldn't pull myself out of and it all seemed ridiculously absurd. Rick had stopped rubbing and was looking at me like I'd lost it—which seemed pretty funny too. "Oh, that was good," I said when I was finally able to bring myself under control.

"It wasn't that funny," said Rick.

I started to giggle a little again. "You have no idea. I really needed that."

"Okaaay," he said, drawing out the word like I'd gone off the deep end.

"Thanks," I said sincerely.

"For what?"

"For being here. I thought you might just dump me off the elevator when we came back."

"Maybe I should have," he smiled. "You deserved it."

"I know. Do you think she'll ever forgive me?"

"I can't speak for her, but she's pretty special. I think it would take more than one outburst to scare her off."

My stomach growled loudly. "I guess we missed dinner, huh?"

"We could make some of that popcorn Mom brought," he said fishing around in the stand next to my bed.

"Sounds good."

Rick went to make the popcorn and stayed late into the evening. By the time he left, things almost felt normal again.

That night as I lay in bed thinking, I remembered someone I hadn't thought about in a long time. One of my earliest memories was of Uncle Paul, my Dad's brother. I'd been out riding my tricycle down the sidewalk when some teenagers backed over me. They were listening to music way too loud and not paying attention as they backed out. The tricycle was destroyed but the way it fell on me protected my head from being crushed. Uncle Paul was first on the scene. He scooped me up and took me to the hospital.

Mom said I was too young to possibly remember that, but I do. He had five kids of his own, but he always had time for me and my siblings too. He was the kind of guy who always wore a smile on his face and loved to joke around.

But the most remarkable thing about Uncle Paul was something I never even considered. He lost both his left arm and leg in World War II. As a paratrooper with the airborne 101st battalion, he fought in the Battle of the Bulge in Bastogne.

He was wounded as he was setting up guns on the battlefield. He saw his best friend blown to pieces. When he had time to gather his wits, he realized his arm had gone limp and was dangling by a thread. He asked a fellow trooper to cut off the rest. But the man couldn't stomach it, so Uncle Paul cut the rest of his arm off himself and tossed it aside.

Germans surrounded Uncle Paul's battalion and he couldn't get out to get help. The Americans were wearing summer uniforms and fighting in cold, snowy conditions with few supplies. After sitting and waiting a long time for General Patton to rescue them, his leg got gangrene from the shrapnel. When they were finally rescued, he asked a medic to go back and get his favorite watch off his arm! By that time things had gotten so bad with his leg that they had to amputate his foot too. Later they found the gangrene had gotten so bad it had spread up his leg. So they cut it off right below the knee.

When Uncle Paul returned home from the hospital, he had a pretty rough time adjusting. Dad remembers him trying to get up the stairs at their house and he broke down and started crying. Dad tried to go help him, but Grandma Devitte stopped him.

"Leave him alone. He's going to have to figure it out for himself," she said.

My dad wasn't sure what to make of that and it must have shown in his face.

"What might seem like a kindness in the short run will be cruel in the long run. You won't always be there to take care of him. If you do, someday when you're not there, he'll need you and won't be able to save himself. The quicker he learns to cope, the quicker he can be independent again."

And she was right. So right that by the time I knew my uncle years later, I never saw him as different than any other fully-abled person. My cousins told me many people did not even realize he lost an arm and a leg because he carried himself so well.

He certainly had a love of life. He never wanted pity or special treatment for his disabilities. I can't remember him talking about any difficulties he had because of his disability. He got himself back into the flow of life. Nothing seemed to stop him. He had an incredible amount of strength and determination. He never complained. He just lived with it. Unfortunately, the gangrene finally poisoned his body and he had a heart attack, just a few years back.

I wished he was here now. Having him by my side would have meant the world. He could have shown me the ropes and taught me more than a thing or two, I was sure. He certainly would have had some good advice. I started to think about what he would have said, until I could feel him standing by my bedside.

"Keep your head up. There's a lot of life out there. Don't give up. Deal with it. You still have a whole body. I didn't and I still made a pretty good go of it. Do me proud and show the world what Devittes are made of."

"I will Uncle Paul," I promised to the spot I imagined he was standing. "If you could do it, so can I."

What a wonderful dream, I thought sadly. Then something deep in me said, *But this isn't a dream. You only have one life. Do you want to spend it like this?*

"No!" came my instinctual reply. "No I don't want to be like this one second longer than I have to."

Lying in bed and hoping to die was nothing but a cop out. I wasn't facing half the battle that he had, but I was acting like it was ten times worse. It was time to decide once and for all. Did I really want to die? Or was I a fighter? Did I have what it takes to make more of myself and my life? The more I thought about it, the more I realized dying would just be giving up. I was healthy considering all I'd been through and I was young with my whole life ahead of me.

I also understood that it would be difficult. It was up to me to get myself out of the situation. Before my accident, I could wish for something and if it didn't happen I'd be happy just getting by. But this wasn't something I could just put on the backburner. It was in my face and it was up to me to make the change and fix it. No one else could walk for me. That was my responsibility and I had to own it.

In order to deal with my disability, I thought about the kinds of things I would have to cultivate to be successful. The doctors could only take me so far. I respected their abilities to treat my physical body, but I wasn't certain they had what it would take to truly heal me. I didn't like their God-like attitudes and the way they went around handing out "life sentences" to patients. They might know a lot about healing, but they certainly didn't take into consideration the soul or will of those they treated. So I made a new rule for myself. I would only surround myself with positive people: positive friends, positive family, positive technicians, positive aides, positive therapists, positive nurses, and most importantly positive doctors.

Positive people were not just yes-men, or those who told me only what I wished to hear. These kinds of people would have a special attitude. Instead of dwelling on shortcomings or pointing out problems, they were the kind of people who would come to me with solutions. Instead of throwing me a pity party or trying to limit my activities, they would encourage me to reach for the stars. They wouldn't spend their time or waste mine placing absolutes on an undetermined future. They also wouldn't instigate negativity of any kind, whether it was putting someone down for their political affiliation, gossiping about a co-worker, or grumbling about the weather. It was all negative and I needed positive energy to begin my healing. So I decided anyone who didn't meet that criteria would have to leave.

I also decided the most important tools in my arsenal would be faith, willpower, determination, alignment, discipline, flexibility, and patience. I still didn't have a specific plan, but somehow knew I'd laid the groundwork for my recovery. All that was left to do was pray.

"Dear God," I whispered into the darkness, "I really need your help. If you never help me with another thing, please help me now. Help me find the strength to be like Uncle Paul. I know this road will be long and hard, but help me to know this injury is not stronger than I am. Help me to walk again. If you do, I promise to use my story to help others.

"If it wouldn't be too much trouble, could you send me a sign that I'm on the right track? Could you send me someone to talk to who's been in my metaphorical shoes? Please, there's got to be someone out there that's been paralyzed and learned to walk again. If you could, it would mean so much. You don't know how much it would mean . . . then again, I guess you probably do. Thanks in advance for any help."

CHAPTER FIVE

ANGELS AMONG US

I was debating whether to call Ellen and apologize when she knocked on my door the next morning.

"Is it safe to come in?" she asked poking her head in the room.

A strand of her fiery hair fell forward, swinging like a vibrant butterfly. My heart skipped a beat and my face lit up. Seeing her standing there was the best gift.

"Yes. I can't tell you how sorry I am. I was such a jerk. I should have never said those things. I'm so, so sorry . . . I . . ."

"Apology accepted," she smiled, tentatively stepping into my room. "I, umm brought something . . ." she said, keeping both hands behind her back. "Or rather a few someones."

I looked toward the door but didn't see anyone. "Who?" I asked, angling my wheelchair for a better view.

She nudged my door closed with her foot. "I checked with the hospital and they said as long as I kept it short," she said drawing a carrying cage from behind her.

Jay and Princess weren't too thrilled with their incarceration, but the moment they saw me, Jay let out yowl of joy.

"Hey Boy," I greeted him as Ellen opened the cage.

He took a couple steps out of his prison and sniffed the air with distaste. I leaned down to scoop him up. All of a sudden my head got really heavy and I had to sit up to keep from tumbling forward. I couldn't believe how weak I'd become in such little time. I used to chase the cats around our apartment like it was nothing. Now I couldn't catch Jay to save my life.

Ellen scooped him up and brought him to me. "Here, sit on Daddy's lap," she instructed him.

"Ellen, I don't think I'd better."

Her face clouded with confusion.

"I mean, what if I drop him?"

She rubbed Jay's soft fur against my face. "Say 'hi' to your Daddy."

Jay purred loudly.

I closed my eyes and relaxed into him. "Hey buddy, I'm sorry I haven't seen you in awhile. But I'm working really hard to get back home to you as soon as I can."

He seemed to understand what I said and gently touched my face with his paw. Meanwhile, Princess had come out of the carrier and was winding herself around my legs. She stood on her hind legs as if asking me to notice her too.

"How's my girl?" I asked, scratching her soft head.

"I think they really miss you," said Ellen. "At night they watch the door as if they expect you to walk in at any moment . . . sometimes I forget and catch myself wondering too." A tear glistened in the corner of her eye and she quickly wiped it away.

"You still want me to come home?" I asked, watching her closely.

She nodded. "Yes, always."

"I'm not the man I used to be."

"I know," she said quietly.

"I don't know if I'll ever be the same."

She smiled wistfully. "I don't think any of us will ever be the same. Change is inevitable whatever the circumstance, good or bad. None of us is ever the person we were the day before."

"Yes, but . . ."

"But nothing," she said rubbing Jay's face on mine. "The parts of you I love the most are still here – your strength, your goodness, your open-mindedness, your kindness . . ."

"How can you say that after the way I treated you last night?"

"I'll let you in on a little secret," she said, releasing Jay and leaning in to me. "I was aware before the accident that you weren't a god and knew the problems that went along with marrying a human."

"Yes, but my problems just got a lot worse."

"And so did mine. I still know a good thing when I see it."

"You're crazy."

"Isn't that why you married me?"

"No, it was for your hot body."

She laughed. "Your superficial act doesn't fool me. There's a man with deep soul hiding in there. I've seen him once or twice. Besides, what if it had been me?"

"What?" I asked.

"What if I'd been the one in the accident? Would you just up and leave me?"

"No, but that's different," I stammered.

"How?"

63

"I don't know. I guess because men are supposed to take care of their wives."

"Seriously? That's the best you've got? Men are supposed to take care of their wives? And what exactly have women been doing all this time? Making pies and eating bonbons?"

I knew I was headed for dangerous water again. "No, of course not. I just meant that men are stronger and women are . . ." the look on her face told me I was not helping my case. "What I meant was, society expects certain . . ."

"I think you better quit while you're ahead," she interrupted.

"Gladly," I sighed.

"You will walk again someday. In the meantime, let me do what I vowed to do and take care if you in sickness."

I rolled my eyes. "I'd much rather pass on the sickness bit."

"I wish you could too. But since that's not possible, let's concentrate on the positive. You are strong and you'll find a way to make this work. That's why you'll always be my hero."

"What if I can't? What then?"

"Your hero status isn't contingent on your walking again. It's in spite of it. I'll love you no matter what. Whatever you want or think is right, I'll support . . ."

There was a loud pop and before I could stop it, my right leg snapped and flew up toward my stomach. It froze in that unnatural position, as if I were doing some weird contortionist move. I stared at it repulsed and in awe at the same time. All I could think is that

I'd finally made the leap to becoming a *Looney Tunes* character. The whole thing was so surreal.

Ellen stared wide-eyed as I tried to push it down. "Holy smokes. Should I call a nurse?"

"Yes," I said between pants as I tried to push my leg back into a normal position. I took a few deep breaths and tried to relax. Relaxing sometimes helped with the spasms.

"Could you massage it?" I asked hating that I was too weak to use the proper force to do it myself.

She nodded, and began working my thigh. "Wow, that is tense. Has this been happening often?"

"The doctors say it will happen more often the longer I go without use of my legs. Sometimes they get so violent I think my legs are going to shoot across the room like rockets."

"Does it hurt?"

I tilted my head. "Not exactly. When it's really strong, I can feel the muscles in my stomach tighten. I know it should hurt. My mind almost convinces me I can feel it."

The nurse came in and took over for Ellen. "Looks like you got yourself a real doozy," she said.

"I thought I'd impress my wife. Maybe join the circus when this is all over."

"That's funny. I'd always figured you for more of a monkey trainer than a contortionist," she teased.

As quickly as it'd come, the spasm ceased.

"There you go, all better," she said, setting my leg back into place.

"Does that mean your legs are starting to come back?" Ellen asked hopefully.

"Sorry honey, this is pretty normal for your husband's injury," the nurse answered for me. "It just starts to happen when muscles are no longer being used."

"Oh," Ellen said and quickly looked down. But not before I caught a note of disappointment on her face. That image stayed with me for a long while after she left. She wanted me to walk so badly, at times I thought she almost wanted it more than me. She certainly seemed stronger in her conviction that I would walk again. Never once did she express any doubts.

As I lay there thinking about my life and all that had happened, I felt different. My 'visit' from Uncle Paul had me feeling a bit more at peace. It was as if our 'discussion' had given me the kick in the pants I needed to push all the buzzing and chatter in my head aside so that I could really focus on what was important.

I'd heard somewhere that the French had a saying, "Become who you are." I never really knew what that meant. It had always seemed kind of silly, but as I thought about it, it really seemed to apply to what I was going through. I'd never stopped to think much about my life until the accident. Life was good and didn't require a great deal of thought. Because I lived a charmed existence, I'd never given much thought to who I truly was. I just took it for granted that I was the athlete with a good sense of humor that could get whatever he needed. Sure, I'd always assumed there would be more to my life somewhere down the road. But that something was always sometime far, far away. And because I chose not to think about it, it never came.

Now I realized that I was kind of asleep at the wheel of my own life. I'd talked about having children with Ellen, but never did anything about it. I thought about finding a meaningful hobby or career, but never did anything about it. If I had died, the world would be no better or worse off than if I had never existed. Besides my family, no one would have noticed my absence.

A chill ran up the little bit of my spine that I could feel. The thought didn't sit well with me. I wanted the world to know I'd been in it. I wanted the world to know who I was!

Then a little voice inside my head said, *But who are you?* I stopped and stared into the recesses of my room, until I saw nothing. I continued to stare for a long time into the nothingness, letting my weary mind rest until it too thought of nothing, remembered nothing, was nothing. It was then that I came to a place where I just was. My only job was to exist.

The trance-like state was a form of meditation in which everything was still, tranquil, and silent. I'd searched for such a place my whole life. Yet I had never known that it was what I'd been looking for because I'd been too caught up in reacting to life.

As I lay in silence it occurred to me that the accident was exactly what I'd needed. It wasn't a punishment or confinement. It was a wake-up call to become an active participant in shaping the rest of my existence. I would never have stopped to look into myself if I hadn't been forced to do so. Like learning to walk again, looking inside myself was one of those things I just had to do for myself. I'd become so addicted to the outer world that I neglected to see myself or understand who I really was. I'd been hungry, starved really, and never realized what I was doing to myself by ignoring the person inside.

The more I stared into the silence the more I understood. There was great wisdom in quieting myself enough to hear who I really was. I just had to be brave enough to stay in the moment and confront it instead of letting my mind wander aimlessly like a gnat flitting from one subject to another. This was more of that deep knowing beyond knowing I'd had about walking again. It didn't come from a little voice in my head and was different from my mind reinforcing thoughts I wanted to believe. This was more like instinct. It just was.

I vaguely remembered my mom mentioning something about the Law of Attraction when I was a kid. She'd come home from one of her meetings at the Academy of Yoga and couldn't stop talking about her new friends, Ralph and Lois.

"They have such a fresh, wonderful perspective on life," she'd said lighting a candle and placing it on the table before her. "Now if I were to tell you that I could bend the flame of this candle using only my mind, you would probably think I was crazy, wouldn't you?"

"That would be a really good trick," I said half wondering if my mom had learned a new magic trick.

"That's what I thought too at first. But then Ralph taught us about focusing our thoughts. If we give attention to something either by thinking about how much we want it or by thinking about how much we don't like it, we are giving it a lot of energy. That energy becomes fuel to make that thing happen."

"But if we don't want something, doesn't that mean it shouldn't happen?" I asked.

"It might seem like it would, but by thinking so much about the thing we don't like or don't want, we're actually devoting all our energy to that thing. You may have heard the expression like attracts like?"

I frowned.

"It means positive things attract to each other and negative things attract to each other. Therefore in order to bring positive things in to your life you must concentrate on positive things, just as thinking about negative things will bring negative consequences."

"What does that have to do with the candle?" I asked.

"The power of the mind draws things to happen. Just watch," she said taking a seat and staring at the candle flame.

I dropped into the seat across from her to watch.

"You attract into your life what you think about most. Believe you can't do something and you won't, but believe you can and you will."

With that the flame on the candle bent at a distinct right angle. My eyes widened.

"How'd you do that?" I asked waiting for her to reveal the secret to her magic trick.

Her eyes flicked to me and the flame straightened out. "I just told you. Power of thought."

I narrowed my eyes. *There had to be more to it than that.*

"Look," she said, fishing a purple mimeograph from her purse. In the book, *Fourteen Lessons in Yogi Philosophy and Oriental Occultism,* Yogi Ramacharaka said:

We wish the student to particularly understand that when we say "Thoughts are Things," we are not using the words in a figurative sense or in a fanciful way, but that we are expressing a literal truth. We mean that thought is as much a "thing" as is light, heat, electricity, or similar forms of manifestations. Thought can be seen by the psychic sight; can be felt by the sensitive; and, if the proper instruments were in existence, could be weighed . . . It is like a thin vapor (the degree of density varying), and is just as real as the air around us . . .

It may be necessary for you to fix this fact in your minds by picturing the mind as sending forth thought emanations . . . think of thought emanations as akin to the steam being projected from a boiling tea kettle.

I stared hard at the candle, imagining my thoughts like a boiling tea kettle. But nothing happened. After trying for several minutes I grumbled, "I can't do it."

Mom smiled. "Of course you can. You do it all the time. You just don't realize it. Any time you want something and then get it, you make it happen."

"But that's not the same. That's not bending a candle flame," I said very disheartened.

"It is," she insisted. "You just have to practice more. When you want something what happens?"

"I don't know. I just go and get it."

"Right and do you believe you can have it?"

"I guess so."

"The same thing works here. First you must believe you can do it. Don't tear yourself down by not believing."

I started to protest, but she cut me off. "Just trust that it can happen. Then what do you do when you want something?"

"I go and get it?" I asked uncertainly.

"Do you spend a lot of time thinking that it's not possible or that you can't?"

"No, that would be silly. I know I can do that."

"Right, so you allow yourself to go get whatever it is or receive it."

"I suppose."

"In order to bend the flame, you must first create the desire for it to happen. Then believe it can, and then allow yourself to have it."

I looked at her skeptically. Then I tried again. I concentrated on wanting the flame to bend to the right. Then I allowed myself to believe it was possible.

The flame flickered slightly right of center.

"There, that's it! You're doing it," Mom encouraged.

For the next several days I practiced moving the flame with my mind. I never got it to bend as far as she did. But I'm certain I moved it a couple of times.

Remembering the flame reaffirmed my vow to stay positive and surround myself with positive people. It just all seemed to click. If I could move an inconsequential flame, I could certainly reach deep within and teach my body to walk again.

The very next day, an important piece of the puzzle walked into my room. Dave, one of my fellow Eagle brothers, stopped by. We'd hung out casually in the past. He brought the first computer to the club and even knew how to work it. Back in those days that was quite a feat considering we didn't have search engines, Windows, and all that good stuff. I thought he was brilliant. I also knew he had some back problems, but never connected the two characteristics.

"Have the doctors updated your prognosis since surgery?" he asked.

I shook my head. "They say my condition is incurable, but I believe I'll walk again. I can't explain it, it's just something I know."

He gave me an odd look that I couldn't quite place.

"I know it sounds a little crazy, but this thing is bigger than me. I know it will happen."

"You don't have to explain it to me," he said. "I get it. I was in a car accident a lot like yours several years ago."

I looked at him in surprise. He'd never mentioned it before.

"I broke my back too. My spine was severed and I was paralyzed below the waist. They told me I'd never walk again, but I refused to listen. I believe that when emotions are strong, they create desires. They are a mirror of what you attract into your life."

He had me at broken back, but my ears perked even more when I heard this. He was talking about the very thing I was feeling. I leaned in closer, intent on his every word.

"The way you feel helps you to know exactly what you're attracting into your life and if it's right for you or not. When you feel happy, content, blissful, you know you're on the right track. But when you feel

angry, irritated, or sad for instance, you know you're
not doing what is right for you."

"When the doctors gave me an ultimatum, I knew it
wasn't right for me. In those first couple of minutes and
hours, their words were overpowering. I was engulfed
in sorrow and despair and I knew it couldn't possibly
be good for me. The problem is that when something
like that happens, it's so overpowering that you can't
automatically will yourself into a better spot. It's like
being attacked by a whole school of piranhas. One or
two you can fight off, but a whole school could easily
be the death of you."

"So what did you do?"

"I knew that, to get to a better place emotionally, I
had to go fishing. I might need a net to scoop up all the
piranhas, but I could knock them out one by one."

I gave him a confused look.

"I couldn't go from devastated to on top of the
world immediately, but I could fish for something a
little better. Instead of feeling devastated I reached for
something a little better than guilt over not wearing
my seatbelt. Boom! I snagged one of those piranhas
and stopped it from feeding on me. Then I started to
think about how stupid I'd been and worked myself
up to anger. Boom! Another piranha disappeared.
From there I worked myself up to worrying about
my future, then being disappointed with my progress
and impatient with myself for things not happening a
quickly as I would have liked. Boom, boom, boom,
the negativity fell away, each time being replaced by
something a little better until I started to feel content,
and even happy again."

"Yes, but . . . those are just emotions. How did you fix your body?"

"They're never just emotions, those are energy indicators. Until you're in a good place mentally, it's very difficult to heal physically because you're sending your body mixed messages. You aren't just your mind or just your body, you're a balance of both. In order to be a whole person you have to exercise both. Just like a car has to be in alignment to drive straight, you have to be in alignment to heal and live happily."

"Ok, that makes sense, but I still don't see how that really helped you to walk."

"Only you know what you feel. Others can sympathize and may tell you with the best of intentions what they think is best for you. But the problem is that they can only look at things from their perspective. They only have their own experiences to draw upon and so what they end up telling you about is what has worked best for them. They can't separate from themselves enough to tell you what's best for you, only what would be best for them if they were you. Sometimes their advice is sound and might work for you too, other times it doesn't. That's why it's up to you to check in with your emotions and determine whether it's a good plan for you and consciously decide how to proceed."

"Okay, but what if it doesn't work? There are lots of things in life that I wanted that I didn't get."

"Then you must not have really wanted them bad enough."

"Well sure I did."

"Like what?"

"I don't know. Like being Michael Jordan."

"Did you go to the park and practice your jump shot every day?"

"Well no."

"Then you didn't really want it bad enough, did you?"

I looked at him. "But I've always wanted to be like Mike."

"No you don't. Not really or you would have done whatever it takes to be like Mike. You only fantasized about it. That's what most people do. We say we want things, but when it comes right down to it, we don't really apply ourselves to get them. If you say you really want to play basketball, what do you do?"

"I go play."

"Right. But if you said you wanted to play basketball, then stopped to get ice cream, took a couple steps toward the court, then decided to change your shoes and headed back to the car, then jogged toward the court, saw a friend on the benches, stopped to have a conversation, then decided to go back to the car for some water, you might never go play ball. Or if you did finally make it to the court, your friends would have been tired of waiting and left. The conditions would have changed so that it was no longer possible. That's what most people do in life and that's exactly why they never get what they want. They lose focus or let others derail them from their goals."

"So learning to walk again was a matter of staying focused?"

"That and positive thought. I spent a great deal of time consciously telling my body what I expected of it."

"How did you do that?"

"I'd lay in bed and think about each part that was not working properly and imagine it healing and working as it should. I'd practice the moves over and over in my head. I made an appointment with myself to do it several times a day as if I was in training and going to the gym."

"So you just imagined it all?"

He smiled. "It was more than imagination, but that's a good place to start. Positive thought is extremely powerful. Do you know athletes use it all the time?"

I laughed.

"No, I'm serious, they do. Olympic ski racer, Jean-Claude Killy, was injured before one of his big races so he couldn't physically practice. Do you know what he did? He visualized his practices and went on to win what he called the best race of his life."

"But that's just one guy."

"No, it's not. Arnold Schwarzenegger has been quoted as saying that he uses the power of his mind to visualize his body as he would like it to be before he starts each workout. And Jack Nicklaus attributes half his game to swing and stance and the other half to visualization."

I smiled. "Okay, so that's three."

"There are also several studies in the *International Journal of Sports Psychology* on the power of thought in sports. In one study, scientists connected weightlifters to monitors and asked them to imagine they were lifting weights. The monitors registered as if they were really working out even though they were sitting perfectly still!"

"And that's what you did? Imagined that your back and legs worked again?"

"Yes. My doctors couldn't explain it, but I believe that by concentrating on my body like that I created new pathways. I think I rerouted my body's connections around the injury and reconnected my spinal cord."

I stared at him in amazement. The very thought that my thoughts were all I needed to make myself better seemed almost too good to be true. But I had to give it a try. I figured I had nothing left to lose.

Dave suggested an experiment to prove the power of thought. "When I go home tonight, I'm going to send you intense flashes of heat at exactly 10 pm. See if you can feel them."

"Sure, why not?" I agreed.

That evening, I looked at the clock every so often and wondered if he would really be able to do it. I got distracted watching TV, but at precisely 10 pm, a heat wave came over me. At first I just felt a little warm and threw off the blankets. Then it turned to a rolling boil as if someone had built a fire beneath me and set me in a pot. I grabbed a tissue from the nightstand and wiped my face.

"Whoa, he did it!"

"Did what?" asked Rick who was lounging in the nearby chair.

"Dave." I fanned myself. "He said he was going to send me some heat."

"What are you talking about?"

Before I could answer, the phone rang.

"Did you feel it?" asked Dave.

"Yes! That was awesome. How did you do it?"

"Dude, you did it. That's the power of the subliminal mind. Positive thought will help you tremendously, don't forget that."

"But how . . ."

"Start sending messages to your body, you won't be disappointed."

I later asked a mutual friend if he knew Dave had been in a car accident. He said he'd never heard about it. I only saw Dave one other time before life took us in different directions. I never asked if his story was true. The important thing was he got me to think differently and that made all the difference.

The following day I got notice from the University of Washington Hospital that I had been accepted into its rehab program. This was especially exciting because it specialized in spinal cord injuries and had a long waiting list. However, a neighbor pulled some strings to get me in within the next couple days.

Dr. Cancro stopped by as usual to check on me. "You're looking better," he greeted me. "Any changes to report?"

"No," I shook my head.

He moved my toes, pricked my legs, and rotated my feet. But I still couldn't feel a thing. When he was finished, he closed the door, pulled a chair up next to my bed, and sat down.

"What do you think now about your situation? You have not moved anything in a very long time. Do you still think you are going to walk again?"

"Yes, I am dead certain." I didn't yell it or even raise my voice. But there was great power in my words, much different than before. Instead of the whining insistence of an uncertain child, I said it calmly with great strength and certainty.

Cancro's brows raised and a look of alarm spread over his face. He leaned in and lowered his voice.

"Phil, this isn't going to work. You must be realistic. The staff tells me your family and friends are coming in here feeding your false hopes. You need to get the idea of walking out of your mind. To continue this pretense is just cruel."

I smiled and gently said, "I understand your concerns Doctor, but, trust me, I am just fine."

He looked toward the door and back at me. "I am your friend. I want to help you avoid the imminent pain you're going to feel if you don't stop. You don't understand. I've seen this kind of denial before. It always ends the same. In about three months, you're going to crash and then I will have to pick you up off the ground and put you back together. Please, I beg of you. Stop this nonsense."

I placed a hand over his. "I understand your fear, but that is not going to happen to me. Obviously, this is too much for you to handle. You have refused to listen to me and what I need. You've never given me a chance to prove myself. Therefore, I'm going to have to fire you."

A look of shock crossed his face. I don't think a patient had ever fired him. Who fires their doctor? Especially when they're in a situation like mine.

He quickly stood and backed away. "I think you're making a big mistake."

"I need people on my team who believe in me and possibilities. I am not willing to give up and quit, not now, not ever."

"If that's the way you feel, so be it. But I can't support it."

"It looks like we understand each other perfectly," I said.

"Perfectly," he said and walked out.

I think so often people are in such awe of their doctors that they get the roles reversed. They believe the doctor is the boss and they should follow him blindly. The problem with that is, while they have a great deal of knowledge and experience, they are supposed to be working for you, not the other way around. So if they aren't doing what you're comfortable with, they are not focusing on what's best for you. He was not in alignment with what I needed and therefore could no longer act as a part of the team for my cause.

My family fully supported my decision to find a new doctor. Since I was getting ready to leave Valley in a couple of days, it wouldn't be difficult to replace Dr. Cancro.

"Don't worry," Mom assured me. "I've spoken to Ralph and Lois. Lois did a reading and she says there's someone much better on the way that's going to help you do exactly what you need to."

I smiled. "That's good. How are they?"

She shrugged. "As gifted as ever. Lois says to tell you that the accident was karmic. Without a doubt you will walk again, but that you'll always have some difficulty with your right leg. She says you'll be able to move it, but it won't work as well as it used to."

"But it will work?" I asked staring down at my motionless limbs.

"Most definitely. Oh, and Ralph says he's going to make you a special tape."

"What kind of tape?"

"He says it will help guide your recovery. He's going to put all the instructions on how to use it on one side and then do a guided relaxation and meditation on the other."

I was really excited to hear about the tape. It was exactly what I'd been praying for. The fact that it came from Ralph made it even more special. He and Lois lived in Hawaii, where he was a *kahuna*, but he had started the first yoga academy in our region. As some of my mom's best friends, they always stayed at my parents' place when they came to town. They'd even been married in our backyard. Ralph was also affiliated with the Sivananda Yoga Ashram in Rishikish, India.

Ralph and Lois were anything but ordinary people. We believed they were on a higher plane of existence and the fact that they were willing to help me was pretty special stuff. It was like getting help from other-worldly beings.

I could hardly wait for the two weeks it would take for Ralph's tape to be mailed across the ocean. Knowing they were in my corner was a positive breath of fresh air. They helped me see that there were other possibilities I hadn't tried. They reaffirmed my feeling that I would walk again, even though my legs weren't moving yet. I finally felt like there was a light at the end of the tunnel.

CHAPTER SIX

FINDING BALANCE

If a piano and stringed instrument, such as a guitar, were both tuned properly, hitting a note on the piano would cause the same string on the guitar to vibrate. The principle is simple. The piano's sound waves travel through the air and transfer vibrational energy to the guitar. In the same manner, if you've ever been in a clock shop, you will notice all the wall clock pendulums swing in unison. This isn't some fanciful clockmaker trick, but rather a transfer of energy. The wall catches the vibration and everything on it falls into sync.

Our bodies respond in a similar way to our environments. Yoga is a great example of how this energy works for humans. Certain poses are believed to release pent up energy while others are thought to draw in greater, more refreshing forms of energy. So when Stephenie stopped by for a visit with some of her friends from the Yoga Center, they offered to try some special massage techniques to help loosen up my stiff legs and back. I was game for anything that might restore some of my flexibility.

"What do I do?" I asked curiously.

"Just lie back and relax," said Stephenie.

Her friends spread out in a circle around me, each taking charge of a small section of my body. While one worked on my left foot, kneading the heel, then the arch, and ball, another concentrated on my right.

Stephenie and another woman laid their hands on my legs and ran energy through them.

I know it might sound quite crazy, improbable to some, but such an energy transfer has been quite common throughout much of history and is still used in many Eastern disciplines today. The trick to understanding it is to quiet yourself and allow it to come in. In our hustle bustle world, we get caught up in the moment and so distracted by flashing lights, loud music, and the constant barrage of information coming at us from all angles telling us what we must do, be, or have, that we forget our own strength within.

However, there are signs of this energy transfer – good and bad – all over the planet. If, for example, fear or anger reaches an explosive level among a few people, it can spread panic through a crowd at lightning quick speed. People can be trampled or crushed because of it or that negative energy transfer may result in a riot. On the flip side, most of us have experienced the positive energy transfer of a hysterical child calmed by the touch of a parent. There are all kinds of touch therapies today from infant touch, which helps babies to bond with their mothers, to equine touch programs for kids with autism and other developmental disorders.

In my case, Stephenie and her friends turned it into a whole mind-body healing experience. As they worked on me, drawing energy down through their bodies and letting it flow into mine, we did a guided meditation. In it we realigned my main chakras, or a set of seven energy centers. In the yogic tradition, these seven main points are envisioned as circles or spheres, which represent endless energy. Each chakra contains a different type of energy, all of which must be balanced in order for a person to feel whole and healed. The first chakra or root chakra, located at the base of the spine, is red. It deals with our foundation, being grounded, and basic survival needs. The second or sacral chakra is orange and oversees creativity, pleasure, and well-being. The solar plexus chakra, which is yellow, covers issues of self-esteem and confidence. Love, joy, and happiness belong to the heart chakra, which is typically seen as green. The fifth chakra at the throat is often represented as blue and stands for health and communication. The third eye or place in the middle of your forehead just above your eyes is the sixth chakra. It is indigo and relates to intuition and a balanced mind. Finally, the last chakra, which can be seen as either violet or sometimes white, is located at the crown. It deals with the energy of being one with the divine and peace.

"Take a deep breath in," Stephenie instructed. "And release."

We all followed her instructions.

"Good, now I'm going to count backwards from seven to one. With each chakra count, I want you to take a breath and release it, each time becoming a little more relaxed, until you feel so light you can no longer feel your body. Red seven," she intoned.

I took a deep breath and pushed it out in a long, low gush. As I did so, I imagined all sorts of black gunk leaving my body. It wasn't anything from the physical world. It was more like gathering up all the negative crap that had been collecting in me from the first impact of my accident, to the drugs I'd taken, and trauma of surgery, mingled with the drama of a doctor who refused to listen, and my own psychological junk.

"Orange six," said Steph, keeping the pressure of her massaging hands constant on my leg as she spoke.

I gathered another deep breath in my lungs and cleared some more grime from my body. By the time she finished her count, I felt ten times lighter.

"I want you to imagine yourself now floating above the bed. Allow yourself to rise up and float through the ceiling. Float up above the hospital until you're high in the sky and can see all of Seattle."

I saw myself floating high in the evening sky as if I were on a plane looking back at a miniature replication of the city, complete with twinkling lights.

"Now go even higher, until you can see the whole outline of the United States. Keep flying until you can see the whole world. Now float in the tranquility of space for a few minutes. Take in the wonder and beauty of the stars. Imagine that one of those stars in the distance shines more brightly than the others. Make your way toward it. That is your healing place. All that you need to become well is on that star. See yourself landing on it. Take a few minutes to imagine yourself being fully and completely healed."

I imagined a powerful white light encompassing me. It was strong and beautiful and full of great energy. Despite being on a star, it wasn't hot and it wasn't painful. Sparkles of light like thousands of diamonds wound their way up my legs and back until my whole body was luminescent like some kind of alien being and I felt energized.

When Steph finally called me back, I felt the best I had since the accident. I don't think it was just me. The energy in the room was incredible.

"Wow that was great," I said when we finished. "I should hire you to come by every day."

Murmurs of approval went up around my bed as I looked from one glowing face to the next. I don't know what happened. But there was no denying it had been magical.

The following morning was like any other at the hospital with one big exception. I was going to be transferred to University Hospital later that morning! My favorite nurse came in and we said our goodbyes. Before she left the room I asked her to help me roll onto my side.

No sooner had she started to help me turn, than I blacked out. The next thing I remember, medical personnel were frantically working over me.

"We're giving him full oxygen, but he's only taken in 1 percent," shouted a nurse.

I clawed at the oxygen mask. Having so many people so close was suffocating. I had to get away. My heart raced as medical team pushed in on me.

"Come on buddy, stay with me," shouted a doctor shaking me so that my eyes fluttered open then slammed shut again.

I struggled against darkness. They were all so close. I could feel their breath. I was sure one was sitting on my chest. I could feel the weight of others pressing me to the bed, holding me down.

Some one shouted, "Everyone clear!" and the hands flew away.

I coughed and opened my eyes.

"Phil, can you hear me?" shouted the doctor.

I moaned.

"You've had a massive pulmonary embolism."

"Okay," I said closing my eyes. I was dizzy and everything ached.

"Phil, you need to listen."

I opened my eyes again and tried to focus.

"We're going to feed a tube into your arm. It's going to run through your heart and into your lungs to clear them out."

But I was too out of it to sign the consent forms. Lucky, it didn't take long to locate Ellen. By the time she signed, they had transferred me to a room full of peculiar knobs and dials for the procedure. Once I was hooked up like Frankenstein they threw the switch.

I heard a bang and then my body raised up off the table. It reminded me of being in an electric chair. Pure energy surged through my body with such force that I involuntarily contorted to a semi-raised position. It was so intense I thought I might pass out again. When it was all over I fell back to the table breathless and exhausted.

The doctor came out from behind all the knobs and smiled. "It looks like we broke up the blood clot in your lung. You were very lucky, but you're going to have to take it easy for a few weeks."

"What do you mean?" I asked, thinking I'd been doing nothing but taking it easy.

"We're going to keep you in intensive care while you recover. It usually takes about two weeks to recover from something like this."

My heart raced. If I was in intensive care, I couldn't go to University for treatment. I might lose my spot and go to the back of the waiting list. "No, that's not good enough. I need to be out of here sooner."

"Just relax," he said patting my shoulder. "You've been through a lot this morning. I'll be back to check on you later."

Once he was gone, Ellen and my parents came in to see me. "The doctor says I'm going to be here for two weeks," I said with alarm.

"It's all right," said Ellen hugging me. "The important thing is that you get well."

"That's right, sweetheart," said Mom, taking my hand. "University will wait for you. Everything will happen in its own time, exactly the way it should."

"No, you don't understand. I'm not going to be here that long. It's only going to be two days," I predicted.

"Phil, you need to concentrate on getting your rest and forget about getting out of ICU," said Dad.

"But I know I can do it. I know what I'm capable of and I can feel this."

The ICU nurse gave me a funny look. I'm sure she thought it was the drugs talking. But I made a commitment then and there to leave the ICU in two days. True to my new positive attitude, I knew I had to challenge anything that got in my way of a full recovery.

The medical staff was shocked that I'd lived through such a major embolism. Apparently, something of that magnitude killed most people. If it didn't kill them, they were never quite the same. But I was perfectly fine. In fact, I was so fine that I met my goal of leaving the ICU in just two days. The fact that I beat the odds a second time just added fuel to the flame. I was so high on life and positivity that nothing could have stopped me.

"You really need to slow down just a little," said Stephenie when she came to visit me back on my regular unit.

"Why? I feel great."

"Because you're freaking everyone out a little. You're so determined and wound up, they're afraid you're going to crash. Give yourself a break, and ease up a bit."

"Why should I? I feel fine. Besides, it's your fault I had the embolism to begin with."

"What? How's that my fault?"

"Because you guys did such a good job loosening me up, you probably freed that clot from wherever it was hiding. If nothing else, I hold you partly responsible for all that positive energy. I've been flying high ever since."

"Thanks loads. Don't get me caught up in your warped mind. I'm not claiming responsibility for any of your craziness."

"No good deed goes unpunished," I teased.

*   *   *

Due to my quick recovery from ICU, I was allowed to move to University Hospital only a few days behind the original schedule. I'd grown close to much of the staff over the past several weeks. Everyone came by to see me off. Some brought flowers or cards, others gave me small trinkets to remember them by. Some simply left me with words of wisdom.

Henry, my favorite orderly, was especially sad to see me go. "I took care of a guy named Tom awhile back. He was in a wheelchair like you, young guy, real jolly. Didn't let anything stop him. He kept up with his rehab, and in no time he had a fancy van with a lift. He drove all over the town. And boy did he love to eat!" laughed Henry. "Last time I saw him he was fat and sassy as ever!"

I smiled. "Thanks Henry for all your help. I really do appreciate everything you've done for me. But that's not going to be me. The next time you see my face, I'm going to be walking!"

"Sure thing Phil, sure thing," he said as they loaded me up for my cross town ride.

Henry's story really got to me. How could that guy be happy to be in wheelchair for the rest of his life? And the fat and sassy part disgusted me! I never wanted to be fat.

"I can't believe he would say something like that to me," I said to Rick as we waited for the driver.

My brother shrugged. "He probably thought he was being helpful and giving you hope."

"For what? To live as a cripple?"

"To know that you could have a good, happy life."

"I will never be happy until I can walk again!" Storm clouds rumbled just below the surface of my face.

"Relax man, don't make more out of it than was there. Chalk it up to well-meaning but misguided. Besides, it's not like he's the first person to have said something like that to you. At least he was trying to be nice about it."

"Really, who else doesn't believe I'll walk?"

Rick looked at me like I was insane. "Your whole medical team. Dr. Cancro, Dr. Yang, Mary the night nurse."

I was shocked. Mary had always seemed so nice and supportive. "No, not Mary, you must mean someone else. What does the nurse look like?"

"I know who Mary is. She was your primary night nurse, short curly hair, smiled a lot."

I frowned. That certainly did sound like her. "What makes you think she doesn't believe I'll walk?"

"Because she pulled me aside one night and told me that I should accept the fact that you were about as likely to walk as her dead grandmother. She said it was cruel for your friends and family to keep feeding your belief and that we needed to be more productive in our interactions with you so that you could come to except who you are now and move on." He furrowed his brow. "You had to have known, most of the staff thinks you're nuts. They think we're all nuts."

It troubled me that Mary had thought that way about me. In our conversations – and we'd had several – she'd always seemed so supportive. I was beginning to understand just how much I had to thank my family for. Incidents like these really had to test my family, but they'd managed not to let it get to them and had kept the negativity away from me.

"All ready?" asked Ellen, hopping in the back with us.

"Yes, we were just finishing up anyway," I said to Rick.

"See you over there," he said hopping down.

I waved goodbye, and the ambulance took off.

It was difficult not to take what the doctors and nurses thought about my condition personally. It was as though them believing I could never walk again was a personal affront, like I was a quitter or loser, or that

I wasn't strong enough to do it. I also sometimes felt like they confused what had happened to me physically with a loss of mental capacity.

But in stepping back, I realized that I was a unique case. Not everyone has a strong supportive family like I did. Not everyone had the will to fight like I did. Therefore, the doctors and nurses really did mean well. The medical staff had to rely on their own experiences and statistics to predict what was normal for most people. Most had probably seen many patients crash after losing a limb or learning they would never see, hear, or walk again. And so it was understandable that they would become very protective of those they cared for. They saw so much pain that they wanted to spare the little they believed they had control over. They'd been trained to fix a lot of things, but I'm sure that there were many times when they were extremely frustrated when their patients had incurable injuries or diseases. I guess that's why they call them the medical arts. There's just as much art as science to helping patients reach their potential.

So while I did begin to understand their point of view, I really wished they'd see mine—that just as each patient's injuries were different and therefore physically had to be treated on a case by case basis, so are mental and emotional capacities. The way I saw it, the bigger let-down than never walking again was to count me out and never let me try. I could either listen to them, give up, and accept what they were telling me, or I could put myself through the hardest test of my life, push myself to the limits, and see what happened.

The image of Uncle Paul surfaced in my mind again, watching over me and rooting me on. I remembered one time when I was 19 and had flown down to see him in Vegas. He was an accountant for a couple casinos and knew a lot of movers and shakers in town. He'd let me borrow his fancy Cadillac and told me to go out and have fun. I'd been so impressed that he trusted me to drive it. On another visit a couple of years later, when it was time for dinner, he made a call to an upscale restaurant that had a dress requirement and told the maître d' that his nephew was coming down.

"Sonny, do me a favor. Buy him a nice bottle of wine and don't kick him out because he's not wearing a dinner jacket."

Never once did it even occur to me that my uncle had a hook for an arm and an artificial leg. He was just one of the coolest guys I knew. He lived life to the fullest and made sure the people around him did too. I aimed to be like him and wouldn't stop until I achieved it.

As we rode, I realized that this was my first time in a vehicle since the accident. As cars zoomed by around us, it occurred to me that they carried commuters and that I had once been one of them too. I saw the terrain, roads, and freeways I used to travel and wished I could go back in time and erase everything that had happened. The new hospital was one I could see from my apartment. For a moment, I fantasized they could just drop us at home and Ellen and I could go on about our lives as if nothing had ever happened. A deep longing filled my heart, and I began to feel very sad.

That feeling set off an alarm in my head that told me such thinking wasn't productive and would only make me feel worse. I could continue to reminisce about what I couldn't have at the moment, and work myself into worse and worse feelings of despair, thereby delaying my recovery. Or I could shift my thoughts and do something more productive. I thought about what Rick had said about judging myself based on where I'd come from since the accident instead of what things had been like before I'd been injured.

When I thought about things that way, I had made some great strides. I'd died and was revived from a massive blood clot, I really had no more pain, and my back was stabilized and mending. I was no longer bedridden and could feed myself again. I was strong enough to get myself into a wheelchair on my own. Now I was going to a place that would help me learn how to walk again. I didn't know how they'd do it, but I was sure they had the secret to bring back my lifeless legs.

At the hospital, Ellen went to sign me in and take care of admission while a nurse named Gary took me to my room.

"You must be Phil Devitte. You're a T-8," he said.

"What's that?" I asked.

"We classify people here by the types of spinal injuries they have. T's are people who have thoracic injuries or injuries to the middle section of their backs. The number indicates which vertebra is most injured. T-5s through 9s have full movement of their heads, necks, arms, and fingers, but are paralyzed below the waist. We also have C's here who were injured in their cervical region or neck. They have limited movement, what you know as quadriplegia."

"And you put us all in rooms with similar injuries?"

"We find it's helpful for patients to see and meet people with similar injuries. It helps to develop a peer group that understands what you're going through."

I wasn't sure if that was a good or bad thing. There was no way I was going to stay in my wheelchair and I didn't want anyone holding me back. But I was curious to meet others who'd been through something like me.

"Let's go ahead and get you situated."

While he was rolling me down the hall, I noticed there were personal items like pictures hung from the walls, and stuffed animals, afghans, and home blankets on the beds. Patients' clothes and towels hung in the hallway. It looked like more like a dormitory than the high tech facility I'd imagined.

"This becomes like a home for many of the patients and we try to make it as comfortable as possible. Some people spend months or even years here rehabilitating until they're ready to get back to the real world."

We rolled a little further to a large room with six beds.

"Now this here is called The Swamp. It's going to be your home."

My jaw dropped when I saw the place. There were clothes and towels hanging everywhere, dirty sheets covered the floor. A mish-mash of photos, children's drawings, cards, and deflated balloons were taped to the walls above the beds, which were separated by flimsy green curtains. The place reeked of urine, sweat, and medicine. It didn't take much imagination to see why it was called The Swamp.

My heart fell as he ushered me in. It was like being in a military hospital, a far cry from my shiny, new, private room at Valley.

"Listen up everyone," said Gary. "This here is Phil, the one we've been telling you about. He's going to be your new bunkmate so treat him good."

The others watched with curiosity as Gary helped me into bed.

"Your call button's over here. Press it if you need anything."

"Thanks," I said still in shock at my new surroundings. My bed looked clean enough, but I'd have to see what I could do about getting a private room.

"Phil huh?" asked an older guy.

I nodded, not wanting to get too involved, as I wouldn't be staying.

"I'm Jim. That's Joon." He pointed to a Filipino guy, about my age, watching TV. "Then there's Moe over there." A black man with thick white hair waved in my direction. "Zeek's out at physical therapy and Dave's rolling around out there somewhere."

"Nice to meet you."

"So what are you in for?"

"What?" I asked confused.

"I had a surgery that went bad, Joon and Moe had strokes. What are you in for?"

"Oh, car accident."

He nodded. "That's rough." And then launched into a rather graphic story about his injury.

My stomach churned. It was hard enough dealing with my own. I didn't want to know about anyone else's. Plus, the smell of the place was really getting to me. At home I was a bit of a neat freak, so it disturbed me to be thrown into such an unsanitary pit. I turned my head into my pillow and prayed that my room assignment was just a bad mistake.

"There you are," said Ellen. She took one look around and I could tell by the expression on her face that she was thinking the same thing as me. She quickly drew the curtain around my bed. "Well this is . . . cozy," she whispered. "Don't worry, I'll get you moved as soon as I can."

"Good, because I don't think I can handle this," I said squeezing her hand.

"Oh look," she said, pulling Fire Dog from her purse and setting him on my nightstand, "I brought someone to keep you company." She also pulled a few snapshots out of the two of us and Jay and Princess. "I thought you might like to have a little of home close by."

"Knock, knock," said a female voice. A woman with a brown hair and big blue eyes ducked into my "room" followed by a man in a white lab coat. "I just wanted to come by and introduce myself. I'm Lisa and I'll be your primary nurse."

She was so young when she first walked in, I would have thought she was a candy—striper, if she hadn't have told me differently.

"You're not from around here," I said noting her accent.

"No," she smiled. "I'm from Kansas."

"Like Dorothy from *The Wizard of Oz*," I mused.

"Like I haven't heard that before," she laughed. "If you need anything just let me know."

The man with her reached out his hand to shake mine. "And I'm Doug Harmon. But most people around here just call me Dr. Doug. I'll be working with you to get back to your best. I'll be back to examine you in the morning, but I believe there are several more people who'd like to meet you now. May I?" he asked pointing to the curtain.

I nodded.

Lisa introduced Ellen and me to all the physical and occupational therapists who'd be working with me. By the time we were finished greeting each other, my parents, sister, and brother arrived. Because University was located in the city, it was a quicker and easier drive for all of them.

"It only took us 15 minutes to get here," said Mom smiling. "Remember that traffic jam last week, dear?" she looked at my father. "It took us . . . what was it? An hour and 10 minutes to get home?"

He nodded. "At least."

"I can already tell this is going to be much nicer."

I wanted to laugh. Mom was such an optimist that she didn't even seem to notice the overpowering stench of the room or state of filth.

The day had taken its toll on me. After a short visit, I told my family that I was really tired and wanted to go to sleep.

"Oh, I almost forgot," said Mom. "Ralph's tape came for you." She reached in her purse and pulled it out.

"Thanks," I yawned and took it.

While my family visited, Ellen checked on my room assignment. But there was nothing they could do. There was a long waiting list and beds were hard to come by. Private rooms were virtually unheard of at University. So I would have to make do or find new accommodations somewhere else. Since I couldn't do that to my family, I would have to make do.

I was just about to go to listen to the tape and go to sleep when there was a commotion on the other side of the room.

"Turn it down that blasted thing," Jim yelled at Joon, who made no move to do any such thing. "I said turn it down, you Gook!"

"Go to hell, fatso!" shouted Joon.

"Why don't you come over here and make me, you slanty-eyed freak."

Joon dove out of bed and was on Jim in a second trying to stab him with a plastic butter knife.

"Whoa guys, back off," I yelled.

But they ignored me, wrestling back and forth, throwing punches, and swearing like drunken pirates. The others in the room cheered them on.

Under normal circumstances I would have tried to break them up, but I was powerless to get out of bed and help.

"Guys," I shouted again. "Come on, stop it!"

"Are you kidding?" laughed Moe. "This has been a long time in coming. It's the best entertainment we've had in weeks."

It might have been entertainment for them, but it freaked the heck out of me. I hadn't seen a fight like that since I was on the playground in grade school. I pressed the call button.

In a matter of moments, Gary, who had stayed over, Kendra the night nurse, and several orderlies appeared.

They hauled Joon off Jim and put him back in his own bed. After that, all of Joon's food came pre-cut!

"I thought no one in here could walk," I said to Moe.

He raised his brows. "Joon's the only one who's fully ambulatory. The rest of us get around all right, but nothing like that. So far, he's the lucky one."

I asked Kendra to draw my curtain before she left the room and then called Ellen.

"You've got to get me out of here. These people are crazy. I just witnessed a fight."

"Like people shouting?" asked Ellen.

"No, like one guy attacking another. They're all crazy, who knows what they'll do to me in my sleep. Please, you've got to come take me home."

"Sweetheart, I'm sorry but you know I can't do that. We've been over this. University is the best place for you right now."

I sighed. I knew she was right, but I hated the thought of spending the next six months in The Swamp. I was certain I would go crazy like my bunkmates. I hung up and cried.

I still couldn't believe what I'd gone through. I felt very insecure and afraid. Being powerless during the fight just reinforced the fact that I couldn't take care of myself anymore. I was always going to have to rely on others to protect me. On the *Wild Kingdom,* disabled animals didn't live long. I knew if I was put out in the world, I would be eaten alive. I didn't belong there, but I didn't belong in the real world either.

"What am I going to do?" I asked Fire Dog.

But he just sat stoically on my nightstand.

I was extremely tired and didn't think I could listen to Ralph's tape as I had planned. But then I started to think about the fight. I couldn't waste one second working to get out of The Swamp. At least if I fell asleep listening to the tape, I could go to bed with a positive frame of mind.

CHAPTER SEVEN

LIFE IN THE SWAMP

The next morning I checked my body for signs of movement. But nothing appeared to have changed. I was a little disappointed because I felt sure Ralph's tape would help. After thinking about it, I decided that I couldn't expect miracles and had to give the tape some time to work. And so I made a commitment to stick to it.

The guys in The Swamp seemed a little more normal in the light of day. I learned that Jim owned a piano moving company and Joon was living in Chinatown when he had a massive stroke. I met some other people on our wing too. They were a mixture of men and women, old and young, from every walk of life. It didn't seem to matter if they were engaged in dangerous activities or fluke accidents, serious spinal injuries had a way of finding everyone.

I also realized what I'd been through wasn't half as bad as what some were going through. At least I could move my arms and hands. Many of the patients on that floor were quadriplegics. They counted themselves lucky if they could turn their heads and speak.

Later that morning, Lisa took me to have my first shower since the accident. I was really looking forward to cleaning all the grime from my body. There's only so much a sponge bath can do. It felt kind of weird being rolled down the hall in only a towel—kind of like those dreams in which you're naked in public—but I was too excited about getting clean to worry about that. One thing that goes out the window quickly when you have an injury like mine is modesty.

Once in the shower, the nurse turned on the water and started to bathe me. It felt so good to finally feel the spray of warm water trickling down my body. Then all of a sudden I realized I really couldn't feel the water running all the way down my body. I could feel it on my face, chest, and arms, but unless I looked, I would have never known it was touching my lower torso and legs. It was very creepy and surreal. I knew what should be happening. If I looked hard enough, my mind could almost convince me I could feel it, and yet there was nothing.

The elation at finally being clean turned to sadness. I would never be able to appreciate the feeling of being totally clean again.

Feeling drained and discouraged back in my room, I decided to listen to Ralph's tape again. I relaxed in bed, put on my ear phones, and let his words carry me away. Time lost meaning as I worked through his exercises. Near the end of the tape I felt a tap on my shoulder. It was Lisa.

"Sorry to disturb you. You looked so relaxed and peaceful. I hated to wake you."

"That's all right I wasn't sleeping," I said clicking the tape off. "I was meditating."

"Well it seems to be working. Are you listening to music?"

"No, my friend Ralph who runs the Yoga Center made a series of guided meditations for me."

"Kind of like a healing tape," she smiled.

"Yes, I guess so."

"Well, I wanted to let you know Dr. Doug is going to stop by to see you soon."

"Okay, thanks," I said, turning the tape back on to finish my meditation.

I really didn't want anybody to know what I was doing. I knew the doctors and the hospital staff would think that this was something like voodoo and I needed positive energy around me. After all I'd never had any encouragement from medical science so far. I felt it was just better to do my own thing and not hear the doctors' and nurses' skepticism.

It didn't take long for Dr. Doug to stop by. He was about my same age and a resident from the East Coast. Something about his demeanor immediately put me at ease.

"Are you having any problems?"

"Yes, I can't move my legs," I said very seriously.

He smiled. "Yes, I know. I meant anything in the last 24 hours."

"Oh, no I guess not."

"Have you seen your x-rays?" he asked posting them on a light box next to my bed.

"Yes," I said looking at the silhouette of my spine. It was hard to believe the minor imperfection on my vertebra was causing such a big problem.

"To be honest, you're very lucky to be alive. People with this degree of injury don't often survive, let alone do as well as you are. And then to have a major blood clot on top of it? That's why it's so important for immobile patients to continue to have therapists exercise their limbs and keep those clots from forming. It says here you were clinically dead for almost a minute. You could be a poster child for the cause. I'd love to take you around to talk to patients who complain about being rotated and flipped. You're a living miracle."

"Thanks," I laughed.

"No really, you are," he said looking at me in amazement. "You don't realize just how big all that is."

"Oh, I think I do. After the aneurysm I told my doctors that I would only be in ICU for two days. They said that wasn't possible. That it took a lot longer to heal. But I was out in two days."

He shook his head. "You just never know. So how do you feel about things now?"

I blinked. Neither Dr. Cancro nor Dr. Yang had ever asked me how I felt about my situation. They'd only told me what I should feel. "The doctors at Valley told me I'd never walk again. But . . . I don't believe them. I feel like I will. I can't explain it, there's just something inside me that says different."

"Well, we don't say things like that here. You're situation is very serious, but I've learned never to deal in absolutes. Everyone is different and we can never predict just what the human body is capable of."

When he said that, I began to think maybe I was in the right place after all. Despite the stinky, shamble of a ward I was forced to live in, it was the first time anyone in the medical profession had given me a glimmer of hope. He allowed for possibilities and that was all I was asking for.

"Have you noticed any return of function?" he asked as he examined me.

"No, not yet. I check every morning when I get up."

He felt my legs, rotated my feet, and bent my toes. Then he pricked different parts of my body with the pin to see if I had any sensations.

"That's pretty normal for someone with your injuries," he said when I felt nothing below my waist. "Why don't you try to move your big toe for me?"

I closed my eyes and visualized my body just as Ralph directed in his tape. I imagined sending energy down my body to my toe and wiggling it.

"That's good. Do it again," said Dr. Doug.

My eye flew open. "What?"

"I said, that's good. Move it again!"

"I moved it?"

"You sure did. Do it again."

I closed my eyes and concentrated again, flooding my foot with energy.

"Great. That's good, very good."

"I did it?" I asked in disbelief.

"Look for yourself," he said smiling.

I tried a third time and it moved! It was slight, but there was no mistaking it. I'd moved my toe. "Oh my God! I've done it. I've really done it! Thank you, God. Thank you, thank you."

"Okay, slow down, slow," said Dr. Doug grinning from ear to ear. "This is a very good sign. It means that the message is getting through to the furthest part of your body."

"So I will walk again," I breathed.

"Maybe," he said cautiously. "It means your chances have improved greatly, but it's still no guarantee. There's a lot of work ahead of us before we can make that determination."

"But it's hope. It's hope!" I couldn't stop grinning. I wanted to laugh and cry at the same time.

I couldn't wait to call my family and tell them the good news. Some people might chalk the fact that I moved my toe after listening to Ralph's tape up to coincidence. They might say that the swelling in my spinal cord finally went down enough for the message to get through my body. But let me remind you that spinal injuries don't heal like a surface wound in which your skin grows back and everything is normal again. Spinal tissue doesn't regenerate. Once it's gone, it's gone. My doctors had made it clear in no uncertain terms that injuries like mine were permanent and irreversible.

You could also say it was the power of prayer. I certainly had prayed a lot. But I'd been believing and praying for a long time. Nothing had happened before that day. The only thing that had changed was the tape.

In a discussion on the phone with Ralph, he explained that I should use the tape three times a day: in the morning when I got up, around midday, and again at night just before bed.

"Use it like a pill the doctor gives you," he instructed.

He didn't mean to insinuate that the tape was a substitute for medical care, but rather a supplement. In most other countries, the whole body is treated when someone is injured or ill. It makes sense when you think about it. We are not just our legs or arms or eyes, but a total person. When something goes wrong with one thing, our whole body is affected, whether it's the need to remember to take medicine, finding alternative means to accomplish the same task, or the psychological repercussions of dealing with loss. To isolate and only treat one part of the body doesn't make a lot of sense. But western medicine does it all the time, whether it's for financial reasons or our short-term attention spans, something else, or a combination of things, it doesn't really matter. The fact is it seldom works very well.

The tape added the missing piece of the puzzle for me when it came to learning how to walk again. It guided me in the principles of visualization and imagery, something I'd never used before. It taught me the importance of being mentally involved in my own life.

"It's called co-creation," explained Ralph.

"Co-creation?" I'd heard Mom talk about it before, but never really paid much attention.

"Thoughts are things that, when mixed with purpose and desire, create whatever you call into your life. Everything that you need in the universe is here for the taking if you only look for it."

"Yes, my friend Curtis recently said something like that to me too."

"He sounds like a wise man. When something appears just when you need it most, we call it synchronicity. For example, have you ever thought about a friend you hadn't seen in a long time, only to get a phone call from them? Or maybe you were looking for a piece of information when all of a sudden you bump into someone who randomly starts talking about that very thing and either has the answer or knows where to find it?"

"Yes, in fact I'd been asking the Universe for help when Mom told me you were mailing the tape to me."

"Synchronicity. All you have to do is ask for it and it will come into your life if you are open to it. I want you to think of this tape as the cement in your recovery plan. In order to steer a ship around Cape Horn, a captain must be mentally prepared. It doesn't matter how great his ship or navigation equipment is unless he's mentally prepared."

"Okay, that makes sense."

"In the same way, you will never be able to walk unless you see yourself being able to do it."

"But that's the problem, I can't . . ."

"Tutt tutt, you need to erase all traces of cynicism. If you're going to be successful, you have to suspend reality and see the outcome clearly. How you get there is really not the big issue. The journey takes care of itself if you stay focused on the outcome."

I'd heard something similar during a business workshop I'd attended, but never gave it too much thought. At the time, I dismissed it as a bunch of B.S. to psych up salesmen. But now I realized that I just hadn't understood the full meaning of it.

"You wouldn't expect to buff up your body by sitting on the couch and eating cheesy poofs would you?" asked Ralph.

"No, of course not."

"In the same way, you can't build muscles without taking appropriate action, you can't learn to walk without putting yourself in the right frame of mind. If you keep telling yourself you can't right now, it's as good as telling yourself you never will. You need to positively imprint your mind to build the proper pathways in your brain to make your goal a reality."

Ralph visually walked me through seeing energy enter my head as a beautiful light. Then he had it flow down through my body. I pictured it as a white light. This energy drenched my body and flowed from my head to my toes. I saw my injuries and focused this energy around the wounds. I remember visually seeing the healing light wrap itself around the area of the spinal cord where the injury was. I pictured the injury as dark in color at first and as time went on the darkened area lightened up to where it looked pink like the undamaged spinal cord.

The first thing Ralph asked me to do on the tape was to go to my favorite place and relax. I chose an island with beautiful white sand, blue water, and sun shining brightly over my body. I then visualized the damaged area in my back and concentrated on wrapping this area with good nurturing energy. I saw it pulsating all over the damaged area. Then, I saw the area gradually becoming less dark and decayed and more like the natural color of my skin. I put a halo of white light around the damage area. I watched it travel from my brain, down my spinal cord to the muscles I wanted to move. I visualized myself getting out of a chair smoothly and walking like I did before the accident. I enjoyed watching myself walking with Ellen on the beach. I felt the waves brushing up on my legs and the warm sand beneath my feet.

The visualizations were extremely detailed, like being in a 3-D movie. After the exercises, which took about a half hour, I would slowly come back to the present. I'd flip the tape, and listen to beautiful calming music. Listening allowed me to do two things. First, it gave me a break from being paralyzed and opened me up to a larger world of possibilities. Second, it helped me relax, which gave me hope. The Chinese have a saying about paper tigers having hearts of gnats. In other words, they look formidable on the outside, but have no courage within. Listening to the tape helped me to lose my paper tiger once and for all. I'd insisted I could walk, and prayed that I could and, if I reached deep, there was a spark of knowing. But more often than not, I questioned it. I didn't voice it often. But the truth of the matter was I was terrified. Overcoming that fear was one of the hardest things I ever had to do.

The tape touched me in such a way that I released that fear once and for all. Yes, it was scary to think what could happen. But it was scarier to think what would, if I couldn't let go of my fear and allow myself to move forward unhampered.

And so I created a vast library of visualizations. I saw myself crossing the room to speak with family and friends, bending down to kiss my wife, going grocery shopping, doing the laundry, playing basketball, and driving. I even saw myself traveling through the countryside and imagined that I couldn't find a restroom. I saw myself pulling off to the side of the road and taking a leak. Granted that might seem like a funny fantasy, but, remember, at the time I was catheterized. Being able to go by myself at will was a big deal.

Each time I visualized something, I not only noted what things felt like, but how easy it was to do them. I figured as long as I was imprinting these things on my brain that I might as well make them easy too.

The cool thing about the visualizations was that they took absolutely nothing. I could do them, anytime, anyplace, anywhere. It wasn't something reserved just for me. Anyone could do it and it was free for the taking.

I started to listen to the tape religiously. Right after I got up, I'd listen to help me focus on my priorities for the day. If I noticed self-doubts creeping in, it would take care of them too. By midday my energy level would waver after physical therapy. And if things had not gone so well, frustrations would resurface. So I'd take another dose of Ralph's tape. Then I'd imprint myself one more time as I fell asleep each evening.

Sometimes I'd fall asleep with the tape running, but that was ok because my subconscious mind still took it in. And there were many times I would listen to that tape more than three times a day. It just depended on what I was feeling. It wasn't a magic bullet by any means, but what it did was bring my inner power to the surface, by making me consciously aware of my goals and actions.

In addition to the visualization, I also practiced positive affirmations. I'd say things to myself like, *I am walking now. I am running and free of pain just like I was before the accident.* I usually said them to myself right after I finished Ralph's tape. But I also started to say them to myself anywhere and everywhere. At first I whispered them, but people at the hospital looked at me like I was nuts. I think some of them wondered if I'd suffered brain-damage too. So I learned to just say them silently in my head. When I was finished, I always felt stronger and full of self-confidence.

After making affirmations a daily habit, my conscious mind had no alternative but to believe in what I was affirming. You are what you think! My conscious mind was working on my subconscious, saying, "Hey, you better listen! This guy ain't playing. He's for real."

It wasn't long after I got the tape that I came across a copy of Napoleon Hill's book *Think and Grow Rich*. I'd read it before as a business book, but found new meaning when I picked it up this time.

Just a few pages in, it talked about the fact that success is for everyone. The difference is that most people give up before they reach their goals. It went on to say that:

More than five hundred of the most successful men this country has ever known told the author their greatest success came just one step beyond the point at which defeat had overtaken them. Failure is a trickster with a keen sense of irony and cunning. It takes great delight in tripping one when success is almost within reach.

He talked about the fact that 98 percent of people are never successful because they don't have a goal. Of the 2 percent left, only half or 1 percent will be successful because they not only took action but refused to give up.

That reminded me of another statistic I'd heard about 1 percent of the world earning 96 percent of its wealth. And then there was Thomas Edison's quote about genius being *1 percent inspiration, 99 percent perspiration*.

In some strange way, I felt there was a parallel between these 1 percents and the fact that doctors had told me less than 1 percent of people with spinal cord injuries such as mine were ever able to walk again.

To me it was more than a coincidence. It was a message. A sign that I should never, ever give up.

CHAPTER EIGHT

THE QUICKIE

Not long after I arrived at University, I got my own wheelchair. It was a slick, black and white, state-of-the-art number called a Quickie. Unlike the clunky hospital wheelchairs, this one was lightweight and fast. Athletes in the Paralympics used them. Everyone commented on how cool it was and how good I looked in it. I could care less. I was still fully committed to walking again. As far as I was concerned, the chair was just another medical device, like a cast, until I could fully heal.

I had two bodies now. My upper body was fairly normal, except that I was still a little weak from all that I'd been through. Then there was my lower body. Nothing below my bellybutton looked as it once had. In just a month's time, my legs had grown considerably thinner. I hated the way they looked. Not only did they seem scrawny, they often bent at weird angles due to the spasticity. Sometimes I thought they'd come out of my hip sockets, other times the contractions were more subtle, but I found them to be so noticeable that I thought everyone could see how grossly out of whack they were.

While I was happy with my toe progress, life in The Swamp was hard. Part of our rehab was to take care of our own living space and quite frankly my bunkmates were some of the biggest slobs I'd ever met. The stench never got any better—which I was pretty sure was unsanitary and the hospital cleaning staff should at least tend to. The place looked like a rat's nest, which I was sure couldn't possibly be good for morale.

When the guys weren't bickering with each other, they were all right. But for the most part they lamented over their situations, and I just couldn't be a part of that.

Now that I was so much closer, Rick or Curtis came by just about every night. It was huge comfort to have the two of them with me. *If I can't go home, at least I can have a little bit of it here with me,* I reasoned.

"Who's the black guy you keep calling brother?" Moe asked on Curtis' first visit when he stepped out of the room to fix another bag of popcorn.

"Oh, he's a friend from way back. When I was about 10 we moved from Beacon Hill to Central Seattle. His sister threw a brick through our front window and we've been friends ever since."

"Sounds like a nice sister."

"She's actually not too bad. It was just another time. The Black Panthers had their headquarters just a few blocks from our house. So it just wasn't cool for most kids in the neighborhood to be nice to white people. But my parents went to see hers and straighten things out. That's when Curtis and I met and immediately clicked. He's true blue. That first summer we did just about everything together – played basketball, went camping, and fished. We discovered we both liked funk. Tower of Power and George Duke were some of our favorites."

"What about Sly and the Family Stone?"

"Yeah, we like them too," I grinned.

"Cool, cool, you cats got some taste."

"But our taste is eclectic. We like Jimmy Hendrix too."

"Ain't nothing wrong with branching out a little." He gave Curtis the thumbs up when he came back in.

Curtis nodded at him. "What's that all about?" he asked as he sat down next to me to watch the Sonics game.

"I think you just raised my street cred in here," I chuckled.

He smiled and shook his head. "Whatever I can do to help."

One might think being in the hospital for months on end would be laid-back, peaceful, and relaxing. But my days at University were jam-packed full of activities – from constant workouts to examinations, blood tests, x-rays, and intensive therapy. So I really enjoyed my evenings, which were the only time I had to just kick back.

"Go, go, go," shouted Curtis, as the Sonics headed down the court.

"Yes!" I cheered when they made the basket.

"What are you cheering for?" laughed Curtis.

I shrugged. "The Sonics are doing well this year. Tom Chambers is going all the way. They might even win the Pacific Division."

"Fair weather sports fan," he teased.

"Hey, you got to know when to get out."

"No loyalty, absolutely no loyalty."

"What can I say? I stick with winners."

Curtis snorted. "When it's convenient. Name one Seattle team you've stuck with."

"What? I root for the Seahawks."

"Shh, the game's back on," he said turning back to the TV.

When the game was over, Curtis got up to leave.

"Hey man," I said clapping his hand in a tight shake. "Thanks."

"No problem, we always watch the games together."

"No, I mean for all this. For being here for me. For treating me the same and not just being a fair weather friend."

He stooped over and hugged me. "You know I'm here for you. Whatever you need, we're in this together. We'll make it happen."

When Curtis had gone I reached for my Walkman, which was becoming routine, slipped on my headphones, and pressed play. Having people like Curtis visit and then taking a dose of "Ralph" was what I called good medicine. It made some very difficult days go down a lot smoother.

That night I dreamed of walking on the beach with Ellen. I glided along smoothly, feeling the wet sand beneath my toes. From my full height I could look down into her face again. I felt strong and wonderful. At one point, I think I even played chase with her like a kid.

*   *   *

Even though I could move my toe, and believe me I practiced moving it as often as I could, I still didn't really feel it. When I mentioned it to Nancy, my physical therapist, she told me not to worry about it.

"We have plenty of other things on our agenda first," she said.

I was surprised at her brute strength. Built like a drill sergeant, she had no problem picking me up and hauling me around like a sack of potatoes.

"I know I've got long road ahead of me, but don't you think it's odd that my toe is working and not my back? I mean, I just assumed I'd be able to feel the area around my injury first. There's just no rhyme or reason to it."

She shrugged. "Everyone heals differently."

We spent the next few days working on my upper body strength and wheelchair techniques. She was adamant that I learn things like wheelchair transfers, opening doors that swung the wrong way for myself, and negotiating sidewalk curbs.

"I don't see why we have to do these things," I said. "I've told you over and over I'm going to walk again. This is all a waste of time. I want to work on my legs."

"It's not that simple Phil. Even if you do learn to walk, it's going to take a long time. Chances are you'll be back at home before you can do that. You can't expect Ellen to do everything for you. You'll need to know how to get around for yourself."

"No ma'am! No way, once I get out of this thing, I'm never going back," I insisted.

"I know you feel that way now. But you're going to get tired. There will be some situations, especially longer trips and tracks where you'll be grateful for the wheelchair."

"I told you, once I can walk, I'm never going to use this thing again. I don't care how long it takes me to reach my destination."

She shook her head. "Someday, you'll change your mind."

"No," I promised. "I really won't."

But I was glad for the wheelchair a few days later when I learned that I was being released for a short visit home. The most insurance would allow me to have was four hours away from the hospital. It was a February evening close to Valentine's Day.

Since Ellen had a small compact that wouldn't accommodate my wheelchair, she traded cars with a friend. She pulled up to the hospital in this big, honking Continental with suicide doors. The sight of her driving that thing tickled me silly. Once she had me situated in the passenger's seat, she picked up my wheelchair and tossed it in the back like it was nothing. Whatever the mission was, she accomplished it. That's just the way she was. Farm girls are strong people both physically and mentally.

When we got home, she lifted me into my chair. Jay and Princess scampered to the door to greet me. Jay was on my lap in seconds.

"Hi there. How's my boy?" I asked, relieved that I could handle him better than the last time I'd seen him.

It was odd to see the apartment after so many weeks away. It still looked the same—better, Ellen had cleaned it until it sparkled with perfection. But it felt strange. I'd never seen it from such a low angle. Or if I had, I'd never paid attention.

As I rolled into the dining room, I saw two places set and a candle lit on the table. Two of our friends, dressed like waiters from a fine dining establishment, greeted us.

"Good evening sir, madam, would you like to take a seat? The salads will be out momentarily."

I looked up at Ellen.

"Happy Valentine's Day," she said leaning down to kiss me.

"Wow this is great," I said arranging myself at the table.

It was my first home cooked meal and it was beyond delicious. Eating real food again was like an other-worldly experience. It was like tasting everything for the first time. I thought I'd lost my appetite at the hospital, but now I realized it was because the food wasn't particularly good.

I ate until I was stuffed. Coming home was like Christmas, Thanksgiving, and my birthday all rolled into one. I wished I could stay forever, but the time flew by like water through a sieve.

I resented having to go back to the hospital. I went into physical therapy more determined than ever to get home as soon as possible. I pushed myself to the limits in therapy and spent most of my free time exercising mentally either with Ralph's tape or doing affirmations.

After three months of working together, Nancy made a surprise announcement during one of my therapy sessions.

"You'd better bring your energy tomorrow. You're going on a field trip."

"What kind of field trip?" I asked.

"You're going to go downtown and take a bus back to the hospital."

"Oh no, absolutely not!"

"Come on, you don't have to be afraid."

"I said no and I mean it."

"But, you've got all the skills to do this. You're ready."

"I don't give a shit about my skills." I whirled my chair on her. "You're not listening to me. I've been very patient with you. I've done your exercises and I've gone along with everything you've asked of me. But I don't belong in a wheelchair!"

"You act as if being in a wheelchair makes you a lesser person. Is that what you think of people with disabilities? Don't you understand that there are a lot of people who love you? We'll respect you no matter if you can walk or if you have to spend the rest of your life on wheels."

I groaned. "You're really not hearing me. I know my family loves me. And no I don't think any less of people with disabilities. I just know it's not me. It doesn't feel right for me, just like riding a bus isn't right for me. I haven't ridden a bus since I was in grade school and I don't intend to start now."

"But, you're going to need to get around some . . ."

"You're not hearing me," I said very slowly. "That is not me. You say you want me to live as normal a life as possible, but I would never have been caught dead on a bus before my accident and I'm not going to do it now.

"If you really want to help me, you'll start teaching me things I can use, things I want to learn. You see my legs getting stronger every day, but you refuse to give me any tools to strengthen them. I have to do it all on my own. I thought physical therapists were supposed to help, strengthen the body, not ignore it."

"But there's no guarantee you'll ever walk again."

"That may be, but ignoring my progress and refusing to work with it certainly will."

She shook her head. "I don't know. I don't want to give you false hope."

I grabbed her arm and forced her to look into my eyes. "Why did you become a PT?"

"I wanted to make a difference. I wanted to help people recover and become their best."

"Then why aren't you doing that for me? Why?"

"I . . . I . . ." she looked down. "I don't know."

"Hey," I said lifting her chin. "You and I have worked really hard together. You've pumped my upper body up better than Arnold Schwarzenegger. My legs are coming alive. What's that you always say? 'Use it or lose it.' This is my time to use it. We need to start focusing on my legs totally. I need your help and you want to make a difference. I'm going to walk one way or another, so let's do this together."

"But, I usually help people learn how to use their wheelchairs. I don't know much about helping people walk."

"I have faith in you. You know enough or you wouldn't be in my life."

She nodded. "Okay, but I'm not promising anything."

"I only ask that you try."

Nancy bit her lip. "Well, the problem as I see it is that we can see your toes working, but we can't see what else is going on."

"Right," I said not sure what she was getting at.

"So that means somewhere inside you there's a pathway that's working. The nerves in your muscles are sending and receiving signals. They just must be really weak. So we need to find some way to see what's going on. When we do that, we can figure out how best to help them work."

"Okay," I said smiling slowly. "I like it. How do we do it?"

She shook her head. "I'm not sure. I'm going to have to do some checking."

"Okay."

"Okay?" she asked. "I thought you'd give me another fight."

"No, all I ask is that you work with me on this."

CHAPTER NINE

TURNING POINT

It didn't take Nancy long to come up with a plan. Within a couple of days, she introduced me to the biofeedback machine.

"When I hook you up to this, I'll be able to see what's going on in your muscles."

"Will it hurt?" I asked looking at the strange contraption.

"No, all I'm going to do is attach these electrodes to different parts of your legs. Then a very, very tiny electrical current is sent out."

"You're going to use electricity on me and it won't hurt? What are you trying to do? Kill me?"

"No," she laughed. "This really is tiny. We measure it in microvolts or millionths of a volt. Basically, the machine sends out a very low signal and then we can measure your muscle response through these sensors."

"Okay, if you think it will help."

"If we're going to do battle, we have to know what we're up against." She was a bit reserved as she hooked me up, but I could tell she was excited.

"We'll start with your left leg since that's the toe that you can move," she said hooking me up. When she was finished, she stood and faced me. "I feel it's only fair to warn you." She paused and bit her lip.

"Yes?" I prompted.

"It's hard to say what we'll see. In fact, if the signal's weak enough we may not see anything at all."

"Okay, then we'll just keep trying."

"No, if we don't see anything, I won't be able to help you learn to walk. It will be definitive proof. I won't be allowed to help you because it would be a waste of time and resources."

For a quick moment I thought about that possibility, but quickly refocused on what I felt. My objective was to see signals move the marker up and down the graph.

I took a deep breath. "Okay, let's go for it."

"Good luck," she said turning the machine on. "Now when I say tighten your quad, I mean tighten your quad. Give it absolutely everything you have."

I had no idea how I was going to do that. I still hadn't felt a thing. But I figured I could at least visualize tightening it. So I gave her a thumbs up.

"Okay, tighten!"

As we watched the monitor, the graph moved! We looked at each other in amazement.

"Do it again," she directed.

I sent a mental signal to my quad like I had done so many times in my mind. The monitor spiked again.

"It moved! It really moved!" I laughed. "You saw it too, didn't you?"

"Yes, yes! I saw it. Way to go!" She high-fived me.

"Okay now what? What do we do next?" I asked.

"Let's see what else works," she said moving the electrodes.

We worked for the better part of an hour testing everything. Some signals were stronger than others, but everything worked. I was getting messages to every part of my body! Despite my nerves picking up the slight movements, they were still so small that we couldn't see them and I couldn't feel them.

It was so cool that everything I'd hoped and prayed for was confirmed. "This means I'm coming back, doesn't it?" I grinned.

A stern looked crossed Nancy's face. "I'm not a doctor, so I can't say. But it sure looks like it."

I was so excited I could hardly wait to tell Ellen and the rest of my family. I wheeled back to my room at top speed.

Seeing proof of all that I'd worked so hard for reinforced my belief in myself. The phrase 'being in alignment' sprang to mind. Thoughts take form and become things. If we give them enough focus, they can virtually become anything we set our minds to. I had proven it.

In the days that followed, Dr. Doug confirmed that some of my nerve pathways certainly were open. However, he couldn't determine how or why they were.

"But we must proceed cautiously," he reminded me. "There's still no guarantee that they'll become strong enough to gain full mobility."

"I know this is difficult for you to believe, especially since there's no scientific explanation. But trust me, there is an explanation."

I didn't bother explaining it to him, because I knew he wouldn't understand. Ralph had often told me we learn things when we are ready to be open to them and not before. That's why some people pick things up so quickly and other resist. At some level, they're afraid of what the new information might do to their lives. I didn't blame Dr. Doug or any of the medical staff. They'd studied for years and had quantifiable evidence to back up what they believed to be true. To believe in something other than what they already knew, especially something so far out, would send their neatly constructed worlds tumbling down. They would have to question everything they thought they knew.

Achievement is very personal. It's totally up to you. The veil of confusion comes in when we trust others over our own feelings and intuition. We let their influence make up our minds for us. But reality is, there's a wide open frontier out there.

I compare my story to Edison and the light bulb. When the light bulb first came out, people laughed. Who would ever use anything so impractical? After all, they had candles. They were inexpensive and virtually everyone knew how to make them. Light bulbs were expensive. Not only did they cost more than candles to use, but you had to install expensive electrical systems to use them. They just didn't seem practical.

But as you know, the idea eventually caught on. Now we mostly use candles when the lights don't work. In the same way, people thought I was crazy, but someday positive thinking and the effects of it will be commonplace.

Over the next month, Nancy and I worked to improve the signal strength to my leg muscles. The process was much like going to the gym and working out with weights. The heaver the weights, the stronger your muscles become. The biofeedback machine was like the weights. Nancy could control the frequency turning it up to make me work harder or down to give me a break.

The more signal strength I could produce in response, the stronger my muscles became. It meant my nerves were finally starting to heal. Because they'd been dormant for so long, they came back in little flickers. Some days I made much more progress than others.

The odds were still against me, but I was gaining on them. Each step I took brought me one step closer to the big goal. I worked out for over a month and a half on the biofeedback machine.

Around this same time, Dr. Doug suggested that Ellen and I have a conjugal visit.

"What? No," I reddened at the suggestion. "It's not like anything's even working right," I reminded him.

He shrugged. "You've been away from home for a very long time. We find that giving couples the chance to reconnect physically can be very helpful to keeping or even stabilizing a relationship."

"You'd allow us to have sex in the hospital?"

"What you do is up to you. I'm suggesting you and your wife spend a private evening together. We have a private room for families and the staff will leave you alone until the next morning."

"I don't know," I said shaking my head.

"Just think about it," he said.

Later when Ellen came by I related my conversation with Dr. Doug to her.

"Okay," she said.

"Okay? You mean you want to do it?" I asked.

"Sure, why not? It would be kind of fun. I haven't spent the night with you in three months."

"'But, but, I'm not sure if anything works . . .'" I said looking down meaningfully. "I don't think I can, ah . . . you know."

She laughed. "Don't worry about it. Let's just see how things go."

I couldn't believe she'd have anything to do with this. Especially knowing what kind of condition I was in. But it didn't seem to faze her one bit.

On the appointed evening she was there with bells on. The staff ushered us into our private room and closed the door.

A chill went up my spine, when I realized I was alone with my wife and what we were expected to do. I felt a little like a lab animal in some crazy reproduction experiment. I began searching the walls.

"What are you doing?" asked Ellen.

"Just checking to make sure there are no two way mirrors or hidden windows," I laughed nervously.

She shook her head. "They wouldn't do that."

"No?" I asked.

"No," she said, sitting on the bed next to me.

"Oh, you're going to, you're going to join me."

"Of course, that's what a conjugal visit is."

"Look Ellen, I don't know what they've told you, but I don't think I can do anything with you."

Her big, blue eyes widened. "Who says we have to do anything?"

"Well um, no one I guess."

She slid under the covers and cuddled up next to me. "It's just nice to lie by your side again." She took my hand in hers and squeezed it.

I raised our clasped hands to my lips and kissed hers. "You are so good to me."

"You better believe it," she said.

That night I dreamed we were walking on the beach together again. Only it wasn't complete fantasy. She was right there beside me, holding my hand through the night.

CHAPTER TEN

THE LONG CRAWL

The next step in my recovery process was to start strengthening my legs with actual physical exercise. Because I was still much too weak to do more than contract my muscles, and certainly too weak to work with weights or any of the other usual workout tools, Nancy decided I should work out with a powder board.

The powder board was about four feet by four feet. It had short legs so that I could put one leg under the board and exercise the other resting on top of it. Working out with the powder board allowed me to strengthen my very weak muscles because it minimized the full forces of gravity by working out in a semi-gravity position.

I didn't automatically have full range of motion in my legs. When I first started out I could not move my leg on the surface of the board. So Nancy fastened a skate to my leg. The device allowed me to move my leg in a fairly good range. As my muscles strengthened, she increased my endurance by adding small weights to my ankle. The more I could move, the more weights I got.

I finally reached a point where I no longer needed the skate because I could move my leg completely on my own. Then Nancy repeated the process adding more weights to my ankle. At one point she piled so many weights on my ankle that it looked like the Leaning Tower of Pisa.

I started laughing at how ridiculous it looked.

"Come on, keep working," Nancy coached.

"I can't," I laughed.

"Yes, you can. It's not that heavy."

"I know that. I'm afraid it's going to topple over."

She stepped back, took a look, and started laughing too. "I'd never thought about it before. You're right, it does look perfectly ludicrous. But the important thing is, it works!"

And work it did. The powder board was big enough that I could vary my workouts and strengthen many different muscle groups from my hips to my hamstrings and quads.

One evening I was really out of sorts. I hadn't made any progress in therapy and was really beating myself up about it. I was achy and exhausted from overworking myself and I was frustrated that my body wasn't doing what I told it to.

When Rick and Curtis arrived, I was bone tired.

"Come on, let's stretch you," said Curtis when I complained about being stiff.

He and Rick often took turns working my legs, ankles, and feet. They picked one up and then the other, bearing my dead weight. Then they'd rotate my ankles back and forth, side to side.

"Come on boy, work that dorsiflexion," Curtis encouraged.

That was extremely important because that movement caused by the muscle in your ankle is used in walking. If it doesn't work properly, it is very difficult to walk well.

"I am," I said panting.

"Harder."

I was trying, really trying, but it was hard work. It felt like a weight pressing down on my chest.

"Come on, you big sissy, work it."

"You can do it, come on," Rick chimed in.

Curtis bent my ankle more. If I had proper control over my legs I would have kicked him away. But I was powerless to stop him.

"I said, 'Come on.' You can do this. You've done it before," he goaded me.

"I'm trying," I said squeezing my eyes shut against the suffocating feeling.

"Not good enough, keep going."

I felt as if my lungs were going to pop, but he wouldn't let up.

"Push, push, push."

"Stop it nigger! Just leave me alone."

He took a step back and Rick's jaw dropped open.

As soon as the words left my mouth, I knew I'd made a huge mistake. "Curtis, I'm sorry. I didn't mean it." I'd never said anything like that to him ever. I was mortified.

He stared at me for a long time.

"Curtis, I am so sorry. It's just that this is so frustrating and it seems like there's nothing I can do. No matter how hard I try. It doesn't happen. And I know I used to be able to do this no problem. Even a toddler can do this. Do you know what it feels like to not be capable of something even small children can do? I hate it, I hate it, I hate it." Tears brimmed in my eyes. "I hate it man, more than anything in life. And now I've take that out on you. Can you ever forgive me?"

"I was just trying to do was best for you," he said in a low voice.

"I know. And I really appreciate that."

"I'm trying to help you achieve your dream."

"Yes, I know it's for the best. I can't tell you how sorry I am. I will never, ever say that again."

"As long as we understand each other," he said.

I nodded. "We do."

*   *   *

There were other muscles I needed to strengthen that Nancy referred to as my trunk muscles. They were the muscles in my pelvic region that helped to stabilize my body so I wouldn't sway uncontrollably from side to side.

"We need to try something new today," she informed me after several weeks of powder board work. "Since we need to strengthen your trunk muscles some more, I think we should try crawling."

"Crawling?" I asked. "But I thought the powder board already worked my trunk."

"It does to some degree, but I think crawling will be even better. It will build greater strength, plus it will be a great skill to have to get around without your chair."

Mentally this was a huge boost for me. The physical benefits of crawling were incredible. I was using my muscles in the same sequence I would if I was walking. Not only that, but the added weight of my body helped to build additional strength.

Nancy presented me with a pair of knee pads to help in my treks across the floor. It was rocky at first, but each day, I grew a little stronger and made it a little further.

About this same time, insurance required me to take a break from the hospital. In most situations patients reach a point and they just don't get any better. They plateau. When that happens insurance companies say, "Well you're not going to get any better so it's time for you to go home."

But in my case, things were constantly improving. Little by little I was getting better. But because those strides were so small and taking so long, insurance only allowed it to a point. The company decided that I needed to go home for about a week. The idea was to suspend services while I continued to improve so that they would last a little longer and I'd be that much further along to get more help down the road.

While I was excited to finally get to go home for awhile, I was worried about losing precious time in physical therapy. So I set up a schedule for myself.

I was like an Olympic athlete in training. I ate, slept, and drank my goal. I made a sport out of crawling. I designed a course around my apartment, and I would time myself to see how fast I could make it around the course. In the beginning Jay and Princess followed me, wondering what on earth I was up to.

Each time I crawled, I would try to better my time. Soon I was crawling pretty fast and had developed good balance. I think the cats finally decided I was just doing some crazy human thing and for the most part ignored the "training."

"I think we should have my family over for dinner," I announced to Ellen when she came home from work.

"Okay, we can do that," she said.

"I have something to show them. But I want to show you first," I said lowering myself to the floor.

She gasped and started toward me.

"No, it's all right," I smiled. "Just watch." I pulled a pair of knee pads from under the couch and put them on. Then I crawled through my obstacle course at what I was sure was record speed.

When I finished, she was on her knees kissing me. "You can crawl," she said looking into my eyes with wonder. "You can really crawl," she said hugging me.

Within a day or two, Curtis and my family assembled at our apartment for dinner.

"So what's going on?" asked Dad. "What's this about a surprise?"

"Surprise?" I quipped. "You're just going to have to wait until after dinner.

Everyone kept looking at me expectantly through the meal.

"If you're not going to tell us, I'm going to guess," said Rick. "You've sold your story to *Time Magazine*."

"No, he's won the lottery," Curtis chimed in.

"I doubt it," reasoned Steph. "Phil could never keep quiet for this long about something like that."

"Maybe there's a little one on the way," guessed Mom.

Ellen choked on her wine.

"We heard about that conjugal visit of yours," said Dad.

"No," Ellen said turning pink. "I assure you, that's not it."

When dinner finally ended, everyone gathered in the living room. I wheeled myself over to the sofa and took a seat next to Ellen. The room grew silent with anticipation. But I couldn't resist drawing things out a little bit longer.

I turned to Curtis. "Beautiful weather we've been having lately."

"It's not too bad," he answered.

"I thought we were going to have a really cool summer, but things are shaping up nicely . . ."

"Enough small talk," Rick shouted. "Where's the surprise?"

"Yeah, where's the surprise?" echoed Steph.

"Ok you guys you have waited long enough," I grinned. "Ellen, if you would hand me my knee pads."

She reached under the couch and pulled them from their hiding place. My family watched in astonishment as I put them on and carefully lowered myself to the floor.

I crawled the length on our apartment and back with my head held high. As I passed Mom, she put a hand over her mouth and tears sparkled in her eyes. Steph sniffed loudly, and Dad wiped the corner of his eyes.

By the time I finished my lap, I was in tears too. Some might have viewed this as "Poor Phil, look at what paralysis has done to him." I was proud to show everyone how far I'd come. For the doctors to expect nothing, and now to make it across the room under my own steam was quite a feat.

While I was home, Rick and Curtis arranged to take me over to see my grandmother too. Her house wasn't wheelchair friendly, but my brothers carried me up the steps.

I showed her my newly mastered crawl.

She smiled. "I knew you could do it. You've always been a fighter."

"Which makes me wonder how he ever got Altar Boy of the Year," said Rick. "I think he must have bribed someone."

"You were Altar Boy of the Year?" laughed Curtis.

"He was," said Grandma. "He was even in the paper. I think I have the article in that scrapbook over there."

Rick gave a whoop and dove for the book, just as Grandma pulled it out of his way. She flipped it open and showed Curtis.

"See what a sweet boy he was?"

Curtis laughed. "I don't know, looks like Dennis the Menace to me."

"Don't you listen to them," she said, patting my cheek on her way into the kitchen.

I made a face at them behind her back, and Rick stuck his tongue out at me.

"I saw that!" she called over her shoulder.

"Damn, you're grandma's got eyes in the back of her head too," said Curtis.

CHAPTER ELEVEN

ROUND TWO

Being home did me a world of good. Just having normal surroundings and engaging in normal activities made me feel more and more like my old self. I still listened to Ralph's tapes religiously. I really felt they were the key to my unheard-of recovery. So I decided to make copies of the tapes to share with the patients when I went back to University of Washington Hospital.

I was totally psyched about handing them out. Teamwork was drilled into me as a kid. I felt like that was what was going on with my recovery. Everyone was pitching in and things were getting done. The staff took care of my physical needs and the tape provided my mental exercise program.

I started my tape distribution program the day I returned. Rolling down the hall I ran into some of the people I did rehab with.

"Hey Phil," Charlie greeted me. "Heard you got to go home for a week."

"Sure did," I said.

"Is it true that you've started crawling?" asked Buddy.

"Sure am. One of these days I'm going to be walking too."

Charlie raised his brow. "Are you really a T-8?"

"That's what the doctors tell me."

"But we're T-8s," he said motioning to Buddy and himself. "What's your secret?"

"I'm glad you asked. I think it has to do with balanced mental and physical healing," I explained. "I listen to a special tape several times a day that helps me direct my energy."

"Is that some kind of hippy dippy stuff?" asked Charlie.

Buddy flashed him a look. "I don't care what kind of stuff it is. If it works for Phil, maybe it will work for me."

"Here, try it for yourselves," I said, handing them each a tape.

I rolled down the hall, confident that others would begin to benefit from the same process that had worked for me.

When I arrived in physical therapy, Nancy was helping a guy I'd never met.

"Hi Phil, welcome back," she greeted me. "I've got to run up to the front desk and then we'll get started. Hey, you're a T-8. You should meet Mike. He's a T-8 too."

"Hi," I said shaking his hand. "So what're you in for?"

"Skiing accident. I thought I could fly through a tree," he grinned.

"Man, that had to hurt."

"Naw, comes with the territory."

"What territory's that?"

"Adventure seeker. I'm a competitive acrobatic skier by day and I build skyscrapers by night, or something like that."

"So you walk on steel beams thousands of feet in the air too?"

"That's me. How about you?"

"Oh, nothing that exciting," I said. "I just decided to try doing 360s on the interstate."

"Hey, how'd you like the way they introduce us? T-8, T-8, yeah they'll get along," he said shaking his head. "What kind of reasoning is that?"

"Better be careful," I said. "T-8's not just a matchmaking qualification, it's your name too!"

"Exactly," he laughed. "Like who we are no longer matters. It's almost as bad as calling someone white boy or baldy."

"Sorry about that," said Nancy rejoining us. "I had to check on something. You ready to get started?" she asked me.

"Yeah, sure. I'm going to blow you away with my new skills," I teased.

"If you don't mind, I'm going to stay and work out over there," said Mike.

"I don't mind, do you?" Nancy asked me.

"No, go ahead man, knock yourself out."

"That's what got me here," Mike reminded me.

My workout with Nancy went well. I really did impress her with my new strength and skills.

"What a difference a week makes," she remarked.

I'd become so good at crawling that she decided to test me again, and added some weights to my legs.

"Work it, work it, work it," she encouraged, as I crawled the length of the mat and back again and again.

Sweat dripped from my every pore. If I was a washcloth, she could have wrung me out.

143

"And I thought I was hard on myself when I was at home. I forgot what having a drill sergeant does for me," I said only half joking.

"Good job today," said Nancy when we finished for the day.

"Thanks," I said fully drained as I turned my chair back toward The Swamp. I longed for the days when someone would take me down to physical therapy.

"Hey, wait up," called Mike rolling after me.

I slowed so that he could catch up.

"That was really something back there. You're a mad man."

"Thanks."

He shook his head. "I can't believe you're a T-8 too."

"Careful there white boy," I joked.

"No, I mean, I've been looking for someone to work out with who's basically at my level."

"And you couldn't find another T-8? Have you been hiding under a rock? This place is T-8 central."

"Oh, I've met a few but no one who wants to tackle their injuries the way you do."

"Thanks. I just don't think I should be in this chair. I have a goal of getting out of it soon," I explained.

He nodded. "Me too. It's hard to ski from a wheelchair. Hey, don't look now, here come the Bad News Bears."

"What?" I laughed.

"Shh, just act natural. I'll explain later," he said as the floor's platoon of doctors walked past us on their daily rounds. Mike whistled and looked innocently ahead.

"What are you doing?" I laughed.

"I find if you freeze, deer-in-the-headlights style, it makes it harder for them to see you and they leave you alone."

"Why?" I smiled.

He sighed, "Because, they're the Bad News Bears. Most doctors they say things like 'Don't worry, things will get better with time.' These guys wouldn't know how to soften a diagnosis if they were threatened at gunpoint. All they can say is, "We just don't know what will happen," followed by the worst case scenario. Have you ever noticed that? Nothing they say is ever positive?"

"Bad News Bears," I agreed.

Before Mike showed up, I took my recovery very seriously. There was nothing funny about it. Everything about the hospital was icky and I hated it all. But Mike taught me it was okay to laugh about, healthy even. He hated his situation too, but somehow making fun of it made it less horrible.

A week after my return, I was eager to see how people were doing with the tapes. Charlie especially had seemed so excited about the concept.

"How's that tape working out for you?" I asked when I ran into him in the hallways.

"It was cool, it was cool," he nodded. "But I still can't move my legs."

"Well, are you still listening to it?"

"Naw, the batteries for my Walkman died. But it's cool. I'll probably get back to it next week," he assured me.

As I checked around, I discovered a major case of Little Red Hen Syndrome. In the children's tale the Little Red Hen asks for help planting and tending her wheat, but no one wants to. Then she asks for help harvesting it, but still her neighbors have no interest. Finally, she asks for help making and baking the bread, but they don't want to do any of that either. Then everyone smells the delicious bread she's baked and they all come out of the woodwork to beg for a piece. But by then it's too late. She tells them they didn't do any of the work and therefore, won't reap any of the rewards.

I was disappointed when I found that 98 percent of the people I'd given tapes to gave excuses as to why they weren't listening to it. Their Walkmans didn't work, they were too busy with therapy, they didn't have a headset, and it bothered their roommates.

A few did listen for about a week, but, when they didn't see immediate results, they quit too.

I tried to explain that listening involved a great deal of faith. "Faith doesn't have a concept of time," I'd say. "You can't see before you believe, you've got to believe first."

It wasn't that the tape didn't work, it was that they weren't open to letting it work. "If you just give it a little longer, it will unlock realizations you either forgot about or didn't realize you had," I'd say.

I didn't begrudge them. Procrastination was a cornerstone of my world before the accident. I was the king of inaction. Because of it, things often didn't get done and then I'd complain—like the Michael Jordan thing. I wanted to be like Mike, but never took the time to make myself like Mike. *Why should I?* I thought. I was in a comfort zone and really didn't want to rock the boat. I was okay with not doing what was in my heart because I'd already convinced myself it wasn't really possible. And so I became comfortable and lazy about my direction in life.

Wanting to achieve is a very personal thing. I believe everyone that I gave the tape to had the ability to succeed. Maybe they didn't have the ability to walk again—but they certainly had the ability to make great strides in their lives, pun intended. The problem was, they were leaving out key factors in their efforts. They had little to no faith, no discipline, and no patience. I could tell many who listened never actively engaged themselves and participated in the mental exercises. They were wishing for something without taking the needed action.

Feeling a bit discouraged that something that had worked so well for me didn't for most others, I rolled on back to The Swamp. Stephenie had recently brought me a copy of Dr. Wayne Dyer's book *Being in Balance*. I picked it up and started reading where I'd left off. Then I smiled at the words on the page. They fit perfectly with my current disappointment.

Your ability to manifest depends in large part on your own willingness to leave behind the collective unconscious—the collective judgments that make up the totality of human beliefs. The numerous judgments of world belief patterns that you are attached to inhibit your ability to manifest the desires of your heart. Detaching from these beliefs is one of the greatest challenges of your life.

He talked about how the thoughts we permit in our lives impact the outcome of events. Things may not happen the way we'd like them to, but it is because of how we deal with life through our thoughts that things happen to us.

The more I thought about it, the more I realized nothing in my life had happened without me first thinking about it and then taking the action to make it happen. It might have been as small as reading something, listening to the radio, watching the news, or having a conversation with a friend, but thoughts, which lead to actions, were constantly borne out of any of those actions. When something comes up, your brain is searching for what it knows from prior experience. If you get too wrapped up in the past, it's easy to get stuck in a rut and never give yourself the opportunity to move forward.

My friends at the hospital were what they thought, just as I was what I thought. There was a handful of people that did listen to the tape and understand it. They worked with it and saw varying degrees of improvement. But they were few and far between. Most people just didn't get it.

Unfortunately, some of those that didn't complained.

I was just about to ask Ellen to make me another batch for a few more people that were interested when the Bad News Bears paid me a visit.

"We hear you've been handing out tapes," said the chief attending physician.

"Yes, I've made some relaxation tapes."

"People are saying the tapes have special healing powers. You and I both know that's not possible."

I frowned. "They help focus the mind. I believe anyone who uses them can play an active role in directing their recovery. Treating just one part of the body in isolation is counterproductive. You need to balance . . ."

"Mr. Devitte, I appreciate you eagerness to help others, but this is nothing but a bunch of hocus-pocus. There's no real science to it. You can't cure anyone."

"But I'm not trying to cure anyone."

"You're giving them false hope. Do you realize how damaging that is?"

"What? No, it does work. It's worked for me. You've seen the results."

He sighed. "You're what we call a miracle case. Everyone heals differently. You've just been very, very lucky."

"I've applied myself. Thoughts create physical manifestations if you focus your energy."

"Yes, well do you have a degree in psychology or perhaps a medical degree?"

I shook my head. "No."

"Then from now on that tape is banned. You may listen to it as you wish, but please don't hand out any more."

I was about to argue more, but then thought about what Ralph always said. "The universe brings to us what we need. If we're ready, it's there for the taking. If not, we won't see it no matter how much someone tries to explain it."

I think most people still kept the tape. A few just couldn't comprehend it. It didn't make sense to them. But I didn't worry about it. Those who needed it got it and those who weren't ready, didn't.

They were watching me so closely, it wasn't worth it. I felt like I'd be out soon enough. If I wanted to stop by someone's house or see people once they got out, the hospital couldn't stop me or do anything about it at that point!

In the meantime, I'd do my best to get out as soon as possible.

"Bad Boys, bad boys, what ya gonna do when they come for you," Mike sang when he saw me coming down the hall.

"Hi," I greeted him.

"So what's this tape I've heard so much about?"

"Sorry, they've made me promise not to hand out any more."

"Oh contraband! Now I definitely want one."

"Then meet me in the alley at midnight," I joked.

"Shh, here they come. Act natural," he said, making the most ridiculous straight face. "If they see you, they'll break it to you that you're paralyzed and hand you a list of the 500 Top Things You Can't Do."

I laughed and the doctors passed, oblivious to the class clown. "So what's on the agenda for today?" I asked him.

"We're going to work out."

"Is that all?" I asked disappointed.

"Of course not, this is a workout challenge. I challenge you to a rep contest."

"You're on," I said. "Race you to the gym," I said taking off.

We had a series of four muscle group exercises that we worked with weights. When we were both in position, he yelled "Go!"

We both did as many reps as we could as fast as we could – 25, 50, 75 . . .

I thought I might pass out, but I wasn't about to let Mike get the best of me – 98, 99, 100.

"Okay, that's it," I said panting. "I can't do one more."

"That's too bad, because I'm going to do another 100 for my pecks," he challenged.

"Go ahead, look like Arnold if you want. I'm an insurance salesman, not a weightlifter."

"Come on girly-man, buck up."

"Okay, okay," I laughed. "A hundred more for the pecks."

That's how the 100 Rep Club was born. Every day, we'd meet at the gym and challenge each other to do our 100 reps. I did eventually slip him one of my contraband tapes. He listened to it once or twice, but really didn't follow through.

He watched my progress with a bit of envy. "Tell me exactly how you're doing that?" he'd ask.

"It's like I said, it's a balance between mind and body. Just like you can't expect to get buff sitting on the couch, you can't expect to fully heal if you don't align your mental goals with your physical ones."

"Yes, but what are you really doing?"

"Dude, I just told you."

"Whatever, race you to the gym!"

I took off after him down the hall, when he came to a stop.

"Whoa, whoa, we got some duties to attend to—here come the C-seniors."

That's what we called the C injuries or quadriplegics. Mike insisted that as big bad T's it was out job to protect the Cs.

"We're like their sentinels," he informed me. "On the count of three open. 1, 2, 3."

Each of us took a side and swung the double doors back to allow the Cs access to our wing. As we held the doors open we struck ridiculous poses. The Cs paid us little mind, but we found the stupidity of it quite hilarious.

We also amused ourselves quite a bit in occupational therapy. The goal of OT was to help us build strength in our upper bodies and redevelop our fine motor skills. One of the big projects they liked to give people to do was to build these prefabricated bird houses.

"Would you like to build a bird house?" Judy the OT asked me.

"No, I want to build a tool box," I informed her. It just seemed like a more manly thing to do. Besides, where was I supposed to hang a bird house in the city? As a businessman, I'd never had much of a chance to build anything. So when I finished the toolbox I decided to tackle a bigger project.

"I want to build a bookcase," I told a bewildered Judy.

"But we don't have the wood for that," she said.

I shrugged. "Well that's my next project. You said I could choose what I wanted to do and that's it. I've always wanted to build a bookcase."

"You're crazy, man" said Mike when he came in and saw me working away on my masterpiece.

"Oh yeah, well I bet it's going to look ten times better than whatever you're building."

"Would you like to build a birdhouse?" Judy asked Mike.

The look he gave her was so funny, I thought I was going to fall out of my chair from laughter.

"Lady, I'm used to building skyscrapers. I'm not building a damn birdhouse."

CHAPTER TWELVE

RETRIBUTION

Swimming was the next step after crawling. Water took away many of the gravity issues, while still allowing me to work on muscle coordination and other strength-building skills. Nancy worked with me in the water at first, but it soon became my regular activity whenever the pool wasn't occupied for therapy. It was the closest thing I done to walking since January.

Finally, five long months after the accident, I was fitted for leg braces. I was with Dr. Doug when he placed a call to Dr. Cancro.

"Yes, I was wondering if you could tell me a little about Phil Devitte's surgery. Specifically, I'm wondering about the placement of the rod in his back."

I listened quietly as Cancro explained how my back was stabilized and where the rod and wires were. When he was finished I heard him ask, "Has Phil had a relapse? Does he need more surgery?"

"Oh, no, no everything's fine with Phil. We're just fitting him with leg braces," replied Dr. Doug.

"Leg braces?"

"Yes, we believe Phil will be able to walk."

The other end of the line was completely silent. Cancro didn't say a word. Finally he said, "Wish him the best for me."

At that point I knew my former doctor probably felt pretty low. My hope is that he never underestimated the willpower of another patient.

It's funny how things work out. I had many visions of myself going to see him and letting him know he was wrong. I even rehearsed what I'd say. But that day, hearing Dr. Doug tell him as one medical professional to another that I would walk turned out to be all I needed. I released all my anger toward him and immediately felt lighter.

So often the thing about bearing a grudge or being angry at someone is that it hurts you more than it hurts them. People act the way they do, because they are quite all right with their conduct. From their point of view, what they do is just fine. If it weren't, they wouldn't do it. Therefore, it you don't like something that someone does or says, that is your problem, not theirs. In other words, they are fine with it. You are the one who has an issue with whatever happened.

One of the great secrets of life is that the only person you can ever control is yourself. If you don't like something, the only thing you can do to fix it is change yourself. You can never force anyone to change, if that is really not what's in their heart. They may do it for awhile, but sooner or later, they will go back to what's right for them, just as you will gravitate back to what's right for you. That means in order to fix things you may have to walk away from somebody and refuse to participate any longer, or that may mean you must shift the way you look at something.

In the case of Dr. Cancro, I did both. I walked away. But that didn't fix everything. He most likely forgot about me in large part, and went on about his business tending other patients. I was the one who stayed bitter and angry. That didn't punish him. He wasn't even aware of it. I was the one who suffered because I let it get to me. When I was finally able to let go of that anger, things really took off for me.

The leg braces looked like leather and steel robots. Strapping into them was like wrestling an alligator. They each weighed a ton. The right brace went up to my crotch and the left brace hit me right below the knee. At the time, I could barely support my body, but my medical team thought it was time to give it a whirl.

The craziest thing to me was that the braces were bolted to a pair of dress shoes. Who exercises in dress shoes? But that was the hand I was dealt, so I worked with it. Nancy then helped me walk with the aid of parallel bars. When I saw them a chill went up my ever-more-alive spine. They were exactly like the bars I'd visualized myself using so many times! My meditations truly were becoming reality.

I couldn't really walk like a normal person with my braces on. Instead, I kind of practiced swinging my hips back and forth and moving like a giant robot. I took a few clunky steps and stopped.

It was odd finally being on my feet again. It was really cool because I could see how tall I was. Nancy was really short, but she seemed bigger because I was always sitting down. It was neat to see everyone at eye level again.

Within two weeks I moved from the bars to a pair of arm crutches. Having a bit of a vain streak, I'm glad I couldn't see myself at this point or I probably would have died of embarrassment. But I'm fairly certain I looked like one of Jerry's Kids all decked out in what I termed my battle gear. I mean no disrespect. Those kids go through hell and I'm proud of them for the heroic way they carry themselves each and every day. But it is a good visual image of what I looked like.

"Now comes the big test," Nancy informed me after a few days of hobbling around the therapy room on my crutches.

"What's that I asked?"

"Real world experience!"

"You're sending me outside already?"

"No," she laughed. "Just down the hall."

She loaded me up in my wheelchair with all my heavy metal gear and rolled me the end of the longest hall I'd ever seen.

"Has this always been here?" I asked

Nancy made a face. "Of course. You've used it a million times."

With the help of an orderly, they got me balanced and into a standing position.

"How do you feel?" she asked.

"Awkward." I felt incredibly off balance with all the battle gear. I had no idea how I was going to get to the end of the hallway all by myself. I took a deep breath and dragged one foot forward. My legs were so stiff from the braces that they really couldn't bend. I'd pull one foot forward, then forced the other one to follow. Sweat dripped from me as I worked my way along at a snail's pace.

When I reached the other end of the giant hallway, Nancy, the orderly, and few people who'd stopped to watch started cheering and high-fiving each other. I turned with a big grin on my face. My thoughts had become reality. I could walk!

I soon realized the longest hall I'd ever seen was really only 20 feet long. Then, I noticed something strange about the floor. There were literally pools of water spotting the floor. *That's strange,* I thought, *I hadn't noticed them when I was walking.*

"Nancy, what is that all over the floor?"

"That's you," she laughed. "That's your sweat!"

It was a wonder I had any fluid left in my body. I collapsed into my wheelchair completely exhausted. But there would be plenty of days like that one to follow.

Though the Bad News Bears didn't want me distributing my tape, they couldn't very well stop me from talking to the other patients. When I wasn't busy working out, I tried to share my story with as many people as I could. If they seemed open to it, I offered encouragement and explained the principle of balance and co-creating.

One day while I was working my way down the hall, I noticed a new girl. Athletic and pretty, she must have been a few years younger than I was.

"So what are you in for?" I asked.

She looked up at me with sad eyes. "Oh, um, I was rock climbing when the rope broke." She shrugged. "I fell, broke my back, and the rest is history."

"Phil, T-8, car accident," I said holding out my hand.

"Tracy, T-7," she said shaking it.

Over the next couple of weeks, we became friends. I learned from others that she'd been a great athlete, which made me wonder why she was banging around in such a clunker of a wheelchair.

It turned out she didn't have any insurance to cover one. When I found that out, I made a decision.

"You did what?" asked Nancy, when she saw me hobbling down the hall for PT the next day.

"I gave my chair to Tracy," I said calmly.

"Please tell me you mean she's borrowing it."

"No, I mean I gave it to her."

"Phil, that's a 5 thousand dollar piece of equipment."

"I know."

"But you're going to need it back. You're not strong enough to go without it."

I waved her off. "Don't worry about it. I'm not going to need it for long anyway, and she really needs it. This will just give me more incentive to work harder."

When the doctors and my counselor found out what I had done, they called a family conference and brought in my parents and Ellen to reason with me.

"I appreciate, Phil's enthusiasm," said Dr. Doug, "but we really must advise against him giving away his wheelchair."

"But you believe he will be able to fully walk on his own someday, don't you?" quizzed my father.

"Yes, that's a very real possibility, but that's someday, not now. Your son is nowhere near independent on his legs."

"Well, then, I guess he'll have to exercise more and make them stronger," said Dad.

I smiled at him. He'd never been the nurturing type, that was always Mom's job, but his defense of me brought back a moment from my teen years when I'd done something equally crazy. I'd been out with a group of friends. One of the guys, Bobby, had always looked old for his age. So he'd gotten a fake ID and bought us a bunch of cheap booze. We downed the stuff like a bunch of amateurs and immediately got drunk as skunks and sicker than dogs. I'd thrown up on myself and passed out.

When I came to, I was still so sick I could hardly walk. I stumbled home in the middle of one of my parents' dinner parties. He'd taken one look at me and ushered me upstairs. He cleaned me up and put me to bed, without one word of reproach.

"I'll never, never drink again," I promised him as he turned out the lights.

"Oh, I bet you will," he said softly as he closed the door behind him.

When they didn't get the reaction they'd hoped for out of my father they switched to Mom.

"This really is a very poor decision," my counselor said to her.

"Why, because you wouldn't do it?" shot back Mom.

"Because he's not ready. What if he needs it? Insurance won't pay for a new one," she pointed out.

"I won't need it," I said quietly.

"Mrs. Devitte, surely you must understand," appealed the counselor.

Ellen cleared her throat. "If my husband says he's going to walk again, he's going to walk. Thank you for your concern, but Phil's made up his mind and I support that."

My parents nodded in agreement.

"If the girl needs a chair, we shouldn't take it away from her," said Mom. "Maybe you should be more concerned with helping her recover. She sounds like she needs it more."

I was so proud of my parents for understanding and supporting me. If I could have, I'd have jumped for joy. Instead, I settled for wobbling unsteadily to my legs and hugging them.

CHAPTER THIRTEEN

HOME AT LAST

Six months after my accident, it was time to go home for good. After some tearful goodbyes with Lisa, Kendra, and the T-8s, I came to Mike.

"I'm really going to miss you, man," I said clapping him on the back.

"Don't worry, I'm right behind you. How does lunch sound a week from Tuesday?"

"I think I'm open," I grinned.

"See you on the other side," he waved as I got into car.

I would still be going to rehab, but I was finally free of institutional life. When I found my dream apartment with the spectacular view and swimming pool, I had visions of poolside parties and a place to go and relax after a hard day at the office. Now it became my training ground.

Just like Ellen had her routine, I had mine. Since I still couldn't walk very well on my own, my business was getting well. I kept a full schedule.

Every morning before I even got out of bed, I pulled on my headset and listened to Ralph's tape. I wanted to start the day with my mission at hand, before I got tangled up in living. I wanted to make sure my subconscious mind was always working on what the outcome was going to be.

After breakfast, I'd head outside and walk a specific stretch of pavement in our complex. I'd walk the length 30 or 40 times until I could barely walk another step. Then I'd head inside to the pool. When I was in the water, terms like weightlessness never entered my mind. But that was exactly what the swimming pool was. It was actually better than the powder board. I didn't have to fight gravity at all. All I had to do was concentrate on being me and reaching my goal of walking freely.

From a standing position, I could raise my leg towards my chest. The only other place I could do that was on the powder board. After warm-ups, I'd march like I was in the army. At the time, it was the closest motion to walking I could achieve. I could also do other phenomenal things like rotating my leg in a circular motion or balancing on one leg at a time. I could also extend my leg out from my side in full range of motion.

Being able to exercise in such an environment was flat out awesome. Being in the warm water also lowered my spasticity and gave me the ability to strengthen my muscles without fear of an episode.

I did however have one problem with the pool. The bottom of it was so rough that I wore my feet raw practicing in it! Because I wasn't strong enough in the beginning, my foot would drag on the bottom causing my toes to bleed. I tried bandaging them, but the moment they got wet the bandages would just fall off. I tried wearing socks in the pool, but vanity kicked in because that looked too funny.

Lucky, I progressed quickly and was able to pick my legs up within about a week's time. Talk about war wounds and patience!

I listened to Ralph's tape again at noon right after lunch. This was usually a very good time for it, because after such a grueling workout, I often needed to rest and rejuvenate. Sometimes I would get frustrated and seemed to be at a plateau, but listening to the tape got me refueled.

One afternoon Curtis stopped by during one of my workouts around the apartment. When he saw me panting and covered in sweat he said, "You've got to ease up, my brother, or you're going to wear yourself out."

"I can't," I said not breaking my set of reps.

"Where's that thing you used to use?"

"What thing?" I asked breathlessly.

"You know that board thing. Wouldn't that help?"

"Yes, the powder board would help. But they're too expensive and big for the hospital to send home with us."

He thought for a moment. "You say it's called a powder board?"

"Yes," I said straining to lift my leg sideways.

He squatted beside me. "I think I could build you one of those. If I did, could you still use it?"

I stopped working out. "Yeah, yeah, that'd be great. I could definitely use it."

"Okay then, it's decided. I'm making you a powder board."

And so it didn't take long for me to incorporate the powder board back into my daily routine.

After dinner, I could often be found back outside walking the pavement in our complex another 30 or 40 times. When I was really frustrated, I would get up and walk. I had visions of the braces falling off me Forest Gump-style. Of course the movie hadn't come out yet so I saw it happening to me not him, but it was much the same. Run Phil, run!

I'd often have no energy when I started out on my walks. But as I continued walking, I'd walk harder and harder, taking every bit of frustration out in my steps.

"Come on Phil," I'd tell myself. "With each step you need to pick your foot more, and hit the pavement with a good heel strike."

The more I felt about my situation, the harder and stronger my steps were. I could hear each inhale and exhale of breath I took. I felt the sweat coming down my head and dripping on my toes.

At night right before bed I would listen to my tape again. It was a great way to continue to train my subconscious. I figured it got me this far, it could carry me into the home stretch. My last thoughts were those generated by the tape, so that even in sleep I was at work.

*   *   *

Mike didn't join me for lunch on Tuesday, but he did get out quite soon after that. We went to the gym together quite often. He always pushed for perfection.

"Come on you girly-man. Is that all you've got?" he'd coach in his none-too-subtle way. The problem with Mike was that half the time he'd crack me up so much, it was difficult to workout at the same time.

"Okay, okay, I'll do it for real this time," I'd say between chuckles.

While the gym was okay, it really wasn't my cup of tea. I was a self-starter and do-it-yourself-er. My home workout routine suited me much better, plus I had the added advantage of it always being right there and available for me.

So over time, Mike and I started meeting a lot more for lunch, dinners, and birthdays than for going to the gym. He did gain back some more movement, but nothing like what I was experiencing.

On my second Sunday back home, I felt strong enough to go to church. After being cooped up in a hospital and then a house for so long, it was a little strange to be back out in the real world with so many people.

Everyone greeted me with smiles and hugs and welcomed me back. Father Mark read the story of the rich landowner from Mathew 25:14:27.

In it, this landowner is about to go on a long journey. He calls his slaves to him to watch over his possessions. To the first man he gives five talents, to the second man he gives two talents, and to the last man he gives one talent.

Immediately, the one who had received the five talents went and traded them, and gained five more talents. In the same manner, the one who had received the two talents gained two more. But the one who had received only one talent dug a hole in the ground and hid what he had been given.

Now after a long time, the master came home and settled his accounts. The one who had received the five talents came up and brought the five new talents, saying, "Master, you entrusted five talents to me. See, I have gained five more talents."

His master said to him, "Well done, good and faithful slave. You were faithful with a few things. I will put you in charge of many things; enter into the joy of your master."

The slave with two talents approached his master and said, "Master, you entrusted two talents to me. See, I have gained two more talents."

His master said to him, "Well done, good and faithful slave. You were faithful with a few things, I will put you in charge of many things; enter into the joy of your master."

Finally, the slave with one talent came to see his master and said, "Master, I knew you to be a hard man, reaping where you did not sow and gathering where you scattered no seed. And I was afraid, and went away and hid your talent in the ground. See, you have what is yours."

But his master said, "You wicked, lazy slave, you knew that I reap where I did not sow and gather where I scattered no seed. Then you ought to have put my money in the bank, and on my arrival I would have received my money back with interest."

Therefore, he took away the talent away from him, and gave it to the one who had the ten talents.

"For to everyone who has, more shall be given, and he will have an abundance; but from the one who does not have, even what he does have shall be taken away," said Father Mark.

He looked out over the congregation as he started his homily and said, "That master was a pretty strict

one don't you think? But it is true. The more we use
our talents the more abundance we will receive."

The story really hit home with me and I smiled to
myself. I'd gotten a pretty good return on my invested
talents. If I had squandered them as the doctors thought
I should have, I doubted I would be sitting where I
was.

Father Mark ended with, "Go out and use your
talents. Create something wonderful for your life."

When the service was over, I went to thank him for
the message. "That was a really great homily," I said
shaking his hand.

"I thought you might like it," he said patting me on
the back. "When I heard you'd be back I wanted to do
something special for you.

"Thanks, I really enjoyed it," I said grinning.

Father Mark's message inspired me to keep using
my talents to their fullest capacity. Not long after I
moved home, I also started taking driving lessons at
the University of Washington Stadium parking lot.

"Are you up for this?" asked Ellen when she
dropped me off.

I nodded. "It's now or never. I want my old life
back and driving is a part of it."

She bit her lip. "You don't think it's going to trigger
any trauma?"

"Why should it? I've driven for 11 years without a
problem. The accident was just a fluke."

A woman who reminded me a lot of Stevie Nicks
came rolling up to us in a driver's ed car. She rolled
down the window. "Hey there are you Phil?"

I nodded.

"I'm Tricia, your driving instructor." She leaned over and popped the door. "Climb on in."

I looked back at Ellen with a "here goes" expression on my face.

She smiled back and waved. "Good luck!"

"So instead of brake and accelerator pedals, this car has handbrakes," explained Tricia. "Want to try it out?" she asked after she'd explained where everything was.

The idea of driving with my hands was totally foreign to me. Aside from an occasional game of Pong, there weren't many video games when I was a kid. So I didn't have the hand-eye coordination most kids do today.

"Let's give it a whirl," I said squeezing the hand control accelerator.

The car jerked into motion and careened across the parking lot.

"Brake, brake," Tricia said calmly, as we headed straight for a family of ducks, who were congregating at the far end of the lot.

I tried to hit the brake with my foot, but then remembered they were up above. I looked around blindly for the brake, but hit the windshield wiper instead. I tried another lever and think I may have hit the lights as we sailed full speed ahead. All the while I couldn't stop myself from trying to hit the brake with my foot.

Tricia smoothly applied the instructor's brakes and brought the car to a stop in a flurry of feathers and squawks. "Okay, so you're a little rusty. That's all right. We'll get there. Do you want me to review the hand gears again?"

I shook my head. "They just don't make sense to me. I wish I could just drive the old way."

"You know, you just might be able to," she said. "Your left leg seems strong enough."

"Yeah, it's not too bad," I agreed.

For our next lesson she switched me to a left accelerator pedal. It still took me four or five lessons to feel comfortable enough to go take the drivers' test, but it was an all around a better idea for me and the ducks!

CHAPTER FOURTEEN

LIFE AS I KNOW IT

Tears welled in my eyes as I looked down over the sanctuary. I couldn't ask for a better scene than the one before me. Dad and Mom heads bowed together, Stephenie and her brood, Rick and his significant other, Curtis and his, and my dear sweet Ellen, all decked out in their Sunday's best. I had been so very blessed with such a loving, supportive family.

I raised my camera for a quick snapshot before going down to join them. As I headed down the stairs, I heard the echo of Father Mark's voice:

"Christ be with you."

"And also with you," came the response from the congregation.

I tiptoed up the side aisle and slipped into place next to Ellen.

"It's almost time. Where were you?" she whispered.

"Capturing the moment," I winked at her.

Curtis tapped my shoulder as he walked by and we followed.

Father Mark greeted us. "It is with great joy that we welcome Phil and Ellen on this day. God the Almighty, the source of all life, has given them a wonderful gift. What name do you wish to give your child?"

I looked into Ellen's arms at the beautiful baby in the long white christening gown. Every feature was perfectly formed from the soft lashes to the pink cheeks. It still amazed me that we could create something so wonderful.

"We've named her Elizabeth," I said.

"And what do you ask of God's Church for Elizabeth?"

Ellen and I responded together, "Baptism."

"It is right that you ask this for Elizabeth. Mark 10:13-16 says, "Let the little children come to me . . ."

My journey had been a long one and certainly not what I had started out to make it or ever thought it would be. I'd always felt I'd do more than work as an insurance salesman, and the accident taught me what that was. I found an unshakable belief and strength within myself. When I finally had time to sit back and analyze the whole thing, I realized that there were seven principles that guided me through my struggle. As an insurance guy, that was great news, because the principles I followed were universal and the policy never expired.

Because of them, I was successful in my journey. Because of them I also had a commitment to honor. When I promised to make a difference in the lives of others if I could walk again, I meant it. That's why I not only worked with the Spinal Cord Injury Association, but also visited hospitals, schools, and other public venues to share my story.

As I watched Father Mark pour water on Elizabeth, the irony of rebirth was not lost on me. Sometimes we do it voluntarily through a ceremony or commitment to change, but sometimes rebirth comes through great challenge and adversity. While I was still the same guy I'd always been, I was definitely different too. I was better, more compassionate, and much wiser. I had the confidence to believe in myself and literally stand on my own two feet to defend my belief. It had taken a long time and a lot of hard work, but I had made it.

My left leg eventually grew strong enough to shed its brace as well as my left crutch. My right leg moved to a short brace below the knee. Over the next two years the powder board and pool continued to be great tools for strengthening my muscles.

Each time I transferred to a new walking aid, it was precarious. But I got really good at it. It would always start out iffy. At first it made me really nervous, but I would remind myself *this is only for a short minute, I'm going to master this.* It was a risk, but a good risk and I had to take it.

Over time, I replaced the long arm crutch with a walker, then two canes, one cane, and finally none. My short leg brace went from the heavy metal one that attached to dress shoes to a plastic one that I could insert into a regular pair of shoes.

The plastic brace's sole function is to help keep my ankle from dropping. I use this plastic brace to this day, and walk sometimes without it. But over a long period of time, my ankle gets tired and the brace makes it easier to walk properly.

They call my condition Brown Sequard Syndrome. Our spinal cords are made up of highways of nerve cells, each having an important role. Some help move our muscles, others control motor and sensory functions. The nerve highways traveling down our spinal columns intertwine like the stripes on a candy cane.

When my injury occurred, those stripes got all messed up. I couldn't feel anything at first. But then the sensations in my lower extremities came back different than before. My left side has good motor function but can't feel hot and cold. My right side is pretty normal with good motor and sensory function. However, it has always remained weaker. I call my remaining problems my "attitude reminders." Whenever they start to bother me, I remind myself how lucky I am and how far I've come. I made a commitment to myself a long time ago to say to myself at times like these, "No matter what I can still smile."

We all have these moments in life. What we do with them is what's important.

After the birth of Elizabeth, who by the way is absolutely 100 percent my daughter, Ellen and I were blessed again. Nine years later, we had our second daughter Juliette.

Today we're just like any regular family. We laugh and play, sing and dance, do homework and yard work, go to work and school, grocery shop, take long trips (and pee on the side of the road), go out to eat, and to the movies. Sure, we have our moments when we have differences, but we also know how truly blessed we are. We have a deep belief in ourselves and trust our hearts to guide us.

Right now, mine is guiding me to take a long walk on the beach with Ellen!

Phil, after months of surgery and rehabilitation, able to get around on his own with the help of a walker. At left is his wife, Ellen, and behind him is his sister, Stephenie, and brother, Rick.

Two views of the damage to Phil's car from the accident.

Phil proudly poses with his oldest daughter, Elizabeth, center, wife, Ellen, and daughter Juliette, at Elizabeth's high school graduation.

SEVEN ACTION STRENGTHS

I'm sometimes asked to describe the seven action strengths I used in my recovery in more detail. Again, they are faith, willpower, determination, alignment, discipline, flexibility, and patience.

I depended on these strengths as weapons in my arsenal, much as a dragon slayer depends on his sword and strategy. A dragon slayer can't control the dragon. He can't stop it from coming into his territory or breathing fire on his village. But he can control his actions and game plan. He sees himself winning the battle.

When he sees the dragon, he doesn't rush toward it swinging blindly. He takes a step back, waits for the proper moment—perhaps a distraction – and thrusts his sword into its heart.

I believe there is a great deal of depression in the world because people are not living their lives according to their hearts. They get caught up in the negatives of society, falling prey to the expectations and directions of others, instead of following their inner voices and using their inner action strengths.

Faith: Faith is the basis for all other strengths. It's where we get our ability to continue when things look hopeless. It is a natural, intangible energy that all of us have within.

Faith is sometimes hard to understand, because we can't see it. We are brought up to believe in things we can touch and feel. Seeing is believing.

If I had approached my paralysis like that, I would have never walked again. That was the attitude of the experts. Since they didn't have a medical aid, such as a pill, to cure me, then there was nothing out there that could. In a way, they were right. The aids I needed were within me.

It's also important to remember that faith isn't a dimension of time. What I mean is that people conceived of the idea of time. It's a human measurement. Westerners use the Julian Calendar to measure time, but there is also a lunar calendar, solar calendar, Chinese Calendar, Jewish Calendar, and so on. They all measure the passage of time differently. Belief doesn't subscribe to any of them. It is without time.

If I had put my goal to walk on a calendar or time clock, I would have given up long ago. There was nothing fast about my progress. I had to endure a great deal of pain. Looking back, it might seem inevitable that I would walk, but you must remember at the time it was completely unknown. There were many days when I was scared; my legs showed no signs of coming back for a very long time. And then just my toe moved, but it took several more months for anything else to work.

I responded to that fear by telling myself, *"I will walk, I believe, and I have faith."*

Willpower and determination: The synonym of will is determination. I will reference both. We recognize willpower and determination as strengths we use to achieve our goals. When people survive difficult situations they often say they survived "through sheer will and determination."

These strengths are energies developed from any situation that seems to put our goals at risk. They come in our darkest hour when we need help the most. In order to find that help, we must reach deep within. So if you're focusing on things like fatigue, or believing something is going to beat you, you need to refocus your energy and very clearly see the outcome of your desire. Then use your determination and willpower to take action.

People who normally aren't physically strong have been credited with some superhuman feats of strength due to their willpower and determination. How many times have you heard stories about a car jack collapsing, pinning someone to the ground, and a little old lady lifting it up to save someone's life? Or a mother running into a flaming building that firefighters couldn't get into and rescuing her child?

American history is full of stories about willpower and determination. When workers were building the Transcontinental Railroad, they faced a great challenge in the Sierra Nevada Mountains. The grade was too high to go over, so their only option was to blast through. Hundreds of men worked on the project night and day 24/7, but they were only able to blast off 7 inches of stone a day!

The project was supposed to last three years. Luckily, they completed it in a year due to the discovery of nitroglycerin. Can you imagine going to work and no matter how long or how hard you slaved you still saw a stone wall? I can almost feel the joy the railroad workers must have felt when they saw the light at the end of the tunnel. What a testament to willpower and determination!

In the same way, it didn't matter to me that I was dealing with an incurable situation. I used my faith to keep going and my willpower and determination to fuel my action. I reasoned that whatever pushed me, I would push back harder. When I fell, I always had a burning vengeance to achieve more than ever before. There is a Japanese saying that reminds me of this. It says, "Fall down seven times, get up eight."

The more I believed in my outcome, the stronger my willpower and determination to achieve it became.

Alignment: Being in alignment is the art of balancing oneself. I had to be in alignment physically and mentally to achieve my goal of walking. In order to find that alignment, I not only had to have the support of my friends, family, and many caregivers, I also had to support myself. I had to take a step back enough to realize my negative thoughts and energies hurt myself. I had to let go of my ego and all the pain, sorrow, and feelings of being betrayed by God and my body long enough to allow my greater goal to surface.

The process is like two magnets sticking together. A magnet is made up of two energy fields. One side is a negative field and the other is a positive field. When you put the attracting forces together, they may actually fly across a table to connect. Likewise, if you try to stick two like forces together – positive to positive or negative to negative – they will oppose each other. The same holds true when we are achieving a goal. We need both our minds and bodies to work together.

If you want to build a house, it's not just enough to have the physical supplies, you must have the mental know-how to do it as well. I used alignment to put my mind and body on the same page. Not only did I engage in physical treatments and exercises from the medical staff, but I also used Ralph's tape and the support of family and friends to adjust my mental state.

As you can see, alignment works on many different levels. There was the inner alignment, but also the exterior alignment. We all had to be on the same page or in alignment for me to realize my ultimate goal.

I let my intuition and feelings be my guide as to whether everything was in alignment. If I wasn't sure, I would simply take inventory of my feelings. If it felt right, I would proceed. If it didn't, I would rethink my plans.

Emotions are a wonderful built-in indicator of alignment. It sometimes takes some deep inner probing to understand where certain feelings are coming from, but they will never fail you. It goes with the old saying, "You can't fool yourself."

Discipline: Having a goal and being in alignment with it means that you must have discipline to see it through. Discipline was what I lacked before the accident. I believe it was also the most critical element of my action plan.

There were a couple of weak links in my life that were responsible for my lack of discipline. Number One, I never took mental blueprinting seriously before the accident. I was lazy and believed taking time to determine my direction was a waste of time. After all,

I had life pretty good. If something didn't work out for me, I'd just move on to the next thing.

Of course that all changed when I had my back to a wall. I had to change. Discipline is an activity, exercise, or regimen that develops or improves some aspect of your life. There was no room for laziness when action was required.

I called upon discipline to help me exercise like a dog both mentally and physically. The poison of discipline is procrastination. When there were other things in my life that seemed like more fun, such as a TV show, party, or even a nap, I used discipline to keep myself on track. Even when I traveled, I packed my 30 pound weights and made sure to make time to do my workouts.

I also called on discipline when it seemed like nothing had changed or wasn't changing quick enough. I would become very depressed and I would feel sorry for myself. When this happened, I was not in the mood to follow my routine and I certainly didn't have the energy to do my exercises. I could have easily procrastinated and worked out another day. But I asked the all-important question, *"Is this decision/ action in alignment with my goal?"* Of course I knew the answer.

While the concept is an easy one, carrying it out is difficult. I had to take it a day at a time and many of those days I just wanted to throw in the towel.

My daily exercise routine became my Bible. There were changes in my exercises as I progressed, but I never slowed down and I never quit.

The more results I saw, the more discipline I had. I would not go a day without working my plan.

Discipline is the difference between achieving and not achieving goals. It's the motion that makes it all come together. It's the butter of cream.

If you've ever hand-churned butter, you understand the importance of discipline.

Churning is what thickens cream to make the butter. The churning process takes a long time. You must keep churning if you want the butter. You can't do it for a minute or two and come back to it later, then take a break. It's a continuous, forward process. You can't have one process without the other to make butter.

My ability to walk again was a lot like making butter. If I stopped churning the ingredients before I met my goal, I would not have walked again. Discipline is what brings it all together.

Flexibility: How many times have you heard somebody say, "Be more flexible,"?

When you heard that, didn't you raise your defenses? I always did. I always equated flexibility with giving something up. I thought it was a weakness.

I wanted to recover on my terms in the time that I wanted, but paralysis could care less what I wanted. It had its own agenda.

I would never have recovered if I wasn't flexible. I had to make many changes. The first change was to recognize the injury itself. I had to realize that the way I used to do things were just that—the old way. If I held on to the past, I wouldn't have been able to work toward the future. I would have given up many opportunities if I insisted on doing things the old way. The past didn't do me any good. So I had to be flexible and realize that my life had changed and that I was on a new frontier.

Flexibility allowed me to fight paralysis with an open-mindedness that permitted me to try new things. If I would have followed my old way of thinking, *"I'll believe it when I see it,"* nothing would have changed.

I had to change my attitude to one of *"I'll believe it before I see it,"* which also leads back to faith. If I had not been flexible, I probably would have worked on the same motion and gotten the same results—nothing. Ironically, being flexible in my thinking allowed me to gain my physical flexibility back!

I had to try many different possible solutions to find what I was looking for. I fell many times trying different things. It was not easy, but I continued to make adjustments until I found the right answer for me. One of my favorite quotes on success is, "Babe Ruth struck out more times than he hit home runs." Being flexible is an important action strength. It helps us make the adjustments that are needed to achieve our goals.

Being flexible doesn't mean giving up anything. It is a strength that allows for other opportunities.

Patience: Some might see patience and discipline as the same thing. But I see patience as the strength it takes to see something through, while discipline is the action to make it happen.

Living out West, I've heard many stories of gold miners quitting on their claims when they were within inches of the treasure. Their patience ran out. Discipline is the action taken when a glitch arises or to continue a process. Patience is the energy to continue on down the path with an understanding that nothing will be exactly as we think it will be. It is a process of weeding many things out to see things through to the finished product.

Often we want to do things in a hurry, but, as I found out when you experience great challenges such as mine, it is impossible to take one step and be finished. It usually takes many steps. That's where the strength of patience comes in.

I equate the strength of patience to what a shock absorber is to a car. The shock absorber helps keep the car steady and from bottoming out when it runs over a pothole. If it were not for the shock absorber, the car would lose control and go off course. Patience was instrumental to keep me from bottoming out and staying on course.

Each one of these actions, faith, willpower, determination, alignment, discipline, flexibility, and patience, is interdependent on each other. Will they work on their own? Yes, to some degree, but if you want true success you must understand that each is a building block for the other and the structure they create is a circle. Patience requires faith and so the process is complete. The circle allows you to use the seven action strengths to roll forward in life.

Whenever you encounter one of life's difficulties, employ the strengths and believe you have a chance. If you never try, you will never give yourself that chance. Life is a game of chance that follows your heart. If you don't follow your dream you will never know what the answer could be. If you follow your dream and work hard at it, you will succeed. If you don't, at least you know you gave it your best, and that is all any of us can ask for.

FOR THOSE WITH MEDICAL CONDITIONS

When I was down and out, I wished I had somebody to help give me a plan. I desperately wanted someone to guide me and share with me how they did it. That, in large part, is why I promised that I would help others if I ever found a way to walk again.

When I talk to patients in the hospital, I explain that when I was in their situation I had similar medical care. I had doctors making diagnoses. I had nurses administering my medication, cleaning my wounds, and bathing me. I had therapists helping me exercise my body. And I had the social workers psychoanalyzing me and giving me advice. So I had a lot of services available. Their help was instrumental in my recovery.

But there was one huge thing missing to complete the circle. And that was me. I was totally depending on their care. I somehow thought they had the magic pill to make me better. I left myself totally out of the recovery process. Until I realized this, I was pretty scared and depressed.

I'd equate what happened to me as similar to the death of a spouse. I'd say to people, "Just imagine you are married. You and your spouse have been married 27 years. You share good and bad times together and you love each other very much. Then one day on your way home you are involved in this huge traffic jam because of a car accident. You see the helicopter rising up in the sky. As you drive by the accident scene, you notice it must have been a head-on collision. The vehicles are so badly damaged you can't even tell what kinds of cars were involved. You wonder how someone could have survived such an accident.

"Just as you get home, you hear your phone ringing. You answer it and hear the doctor say, 'I'm so sorry but we believe the person in the accident was your wife. We need you to come down and identify the body.'

"You can't believe his words. You think *this can't be happening. We just saw each other this morning. This can't be true.*

"You call your best friend and ask for a ride. You know if you drive yourself you might not get there. He takes you and the whole way there you think *maybe they've mistaken my wife for someone else.* But when you arrive to the hospital your biggest fears are realized. Your spouse has died.

"You start reflecting on your life together and realize that you have to get on the phone and make phone calls to family and friends. The next couple days are hectic. People call and stop by, cards and flowers are delivered.

"You must make funeral arrangements, and sign a lot of paper work. Your family calls you up to let you know they are going to stay with you during this crisis. You are never alone and you have plenty of work to do to keep your mind occupied.

"Then funeral and wake come to an end. You go home and your family says goodbye. You turn to go inside and notice how silent the house is. You look around the room and it finally sinks in. You are really alone. Your spouse is not coming home."

My legs were my "spouse" for 27 years. I missed the sensations of hot and cold. I loved my legs and I missed them so. Now all I had were memories.

I saw myself a as a powerless victim. As we know by now, we can't always control what happens to us, but we can control how we react to it. So it is important to take an active role in your own recovery. When you are involved in your recovery, the process works full circle.

This principle can help each and every one of us in our daily lives. You don't have to be in a hospital to apply the concept to your life. Surround yourself with help from others that strive toward the same goals. But don't forget to draw on your own determination and commitment to see your goal through.

Many times when I speak with patients, they have no clue that being mentally involved in their recovery is just as important as is the care of their doctors. The reason why this happens is because we often live our general lives like this. We don't set goals. We depend on the external means or magic pills to take care of us. So when there are obstacles and we don't see an immediate solution, we tend to get distracted or lost. We forget that we are part of the equation for our own success.

The other thing that's important to remember, especially when recovering from an injury or illness, is that it is all right to be completely and totally frustrated. Frustration can help. Understand that frustration can be a powerful motivator to move out of the situations that are not aligning with what you want in life. Things sometimes happen that we just don't understand. Life is life and you just have to deal with the cards that you've been dealt.

Sometimes the reason will be made known to us later. For instance, my paralysis led me into the work

I love—helping others. I wish I could have found it without going through something as traumatic, but if I did, it would not have had the same effect on me. It is all about attitude and not letting it get to you. I concentrate on what I can do and not on what I can't. If I concentrated on what I couldn't do, I'd be attracting negative energy.

Use your frustration as an indicator to power change. Throw that energy into mental or physical exercises that will help you heal. Use it to fuel your determination and move toward peace, love, and happiness. You deserve to have those things. Anything less is not worth it.

VISUALIZATION TIPS

There is a saying, *The mind is All.* It means that everything we perceive, from sights and sounds, to the way something feels mentally or physically, what it tastes or smells like, all forms in our minds. Therefore, we create the world around us as we know it. And if that is true, then we can mold it to our liking if we consciously apply ourselves through visualization.

One of the reasons visualization works so well is that the subconscious mind doesn't know the difference between what is real and what's not. Because of this, it can be used to help virtually anyone achieve their goals, whether it's overcoming a phobia or past trauma, to becoming a better athlete, losing weight, learning a new skill, or even healing yourself.

Visualizing is easy. Anyone who has ever imagined anything or had a dream is visualizing. Your visualization muscles get stronger every time you use them. The more accurate the image you hold in your mind, the greater the chance of getting what you need and want.

There are a couple of things to remember in order to make your visualizations successful. First, always state them in the present. The thing you want or need is now. It's already here with you. "I can walk" or "I am a great soccer player," not "I will walk" or "I will be a great soccer player." If you state your goal as sometime off in the future, you're training your mind to think of it as happening down the road instead of right now. The problem with that is our subconscious only lives in the present. The future never comes for it.

The next thing to remember during visualization is that the subconscious mind doesn't recognize negatives. In other words, if you were to say something to yourself such as, "I am not stupid," what your subconscious hears is, "I am stupid." So phrase your goals positively. "I am smart." "I am intelligent." "I have what it takes."

It's also very important to ignore any little voice in your head that says things like, "yeah right" or "whatever" when you tell yourself that your goal already exists. The secret is to ignore those annoying little self-doubting voices that try to keep you from doing your best and replace them with more forceful voices that help you reach your absolute best.

In fact, there was a study done on this very thing, which was published in *The Behavior Therapist* many years ago. In the experiment, researchers first yelled at a tennis player saying things like, "You blew it!" and "You dummy!" Later, they changed their negative comments to positive ones, such as, "It's okay, just concentrate on the next serve," and "Stay cool, you can do it."

When the player heard the positive comments, his performance improved so much that he more than doubled the amount of games he won! The same thing happens in your head. When you say things like "yeah right" or "whatever," you undermine yourself. Without realizing it, you keep yourself from achieving your goals.

Finally, you must understand that it is not enough to visualize exercises or repeat affirmations without thinking about them. If you do, they aren't going to work very well. To change thoughts and feelings from negative or neutral to positive requires an active mind and plenty of emotion. If you don't get involved and really think about these things, you might as well be reading the back of a cereal box.

The first step on Ralph's tape was a relaxation exercise. I find that relaxing is a great way to create the proper mindset for visualizing your goals. It not only helps to quiet your body, but centers your mind on the task at hand so that you can give your full attention to whatever it is that you want to achieve.

Relaxation exercises can take many forms. There are many such scripts on the internet as well as in meditation and visualization books. Or you are certainly free to make up your own. The following are a few examples of relaxation exercises:

Proper breathing is the key to connecting with our bodies. It helps us to focus our energies on the task at hand and relax deeply.

Either sit or lie down, with your back straight, it doesn't matter which. The point is to make sure your body is properly positioned to receive the full benefits of what we are about to do.

Close your eyes and take a deep breath, filling your diaphragm with air. You'll know you are doing this right when you see your stomach extend. We often get into the bad habit of chest breathing, but if you watch a baby, you'll see their little tummies move up and down as they breathe. That's exactly what you need to do now.

Now focus on what it feels like inside your body as you breathe. It sometimes helps to concentrate on the very beginning of the breath as the air flows through your body, instead of the whole breathing process.

Try to breath normally, as if you were settling down to take a nap. Don't worry about counting breaths to a rhythm, breathing heavier, deeper, or faster. Simply relax and become aware of the rise and fall of your chest.

If your mind begins to wander, release the thoughts and gently refocus it on your breathing. This does take a bit of getting used to, but it will quickly become second nature if you practice.

Breathe in and out. Breathing is one of the quickest ways for us to connect our minds and bodies. As you focus, concentrate on the moment and what you are about to do. This is a special time set aside just for you to reach your goals.

You don't have to do this for long before you feel the positive effects of breathing. This technique can be used whenever you need to relax anywhere at anytime! Breathe in and out, nice and easy.

Continue to concentrate on your breath releasing all thoughts until your mind is a void for 10 to 15 minutes. If simply breathing is too difficult, you may wish to focus on different parts of your body and physically relax them.

Let's start with your head. We often carry a lot of tension in our heads and foreheads that we're not even aware of. Even when we think we're relaxed, we can often relax our face muscles even more than they already are. So pay special attention to this area in particular.

Close your eyes and imagine a white ball of light just above your head. It is warm and beautiful. When it touches you, you melt into its total comfort. See the ball of light entering your body through the crown of your head. As its cozy warmth envelops you, relax the muscles in your forehead. Let them loosen. Loosen the long cross lines that make you frown or scowl, relax the area between your eyebrows that draws together. Feel the light working its magic as it flows down and over your face, coating you in a layer of complete and total comfort. Feel the light as it touches your eyes relaxing them until your lids feel so light you can no longer feel them. As the light continues its downward journey, release all the tension stored in the areas it passes. Let the tension flow down and out. Let your cheeks, jaw, and mouth go slack. Feel the tension draining from the area until your head feels free and light as if it is floating on a cloud. As soon as the light touches a body part, it not only releases all your angers, fears, doubts, and tension, it replaces them with beautiful sparkling energy that leaves them refreshed and energized.

Follow the light as it moves down your neck, releasing all tension in its path, flowing, warm, comfortable, and beautiful. The healing light now moves to your shoulders. Feel it as it drips down them, forcing the tension from them with soft but gentle pressure. Let all negativity stored within them flow down and out, until it evaporates into nothing. Feel the comfort of the light fill those empty spaces. Relax into its tranquility. Feel the soothing warmth as the light trails down your torso and arms, flushing all toxins from your body. See every last bit of tension flowing out your fingertips. Watch as your body is filled with golden, sparkling light.

Follow the light as it continues its journey down your body, washing all pain, negativity, and sorrow from your spine and pelvis. See them light with peace, hope, and happiness.

Let the light engulf you like a cozy down comforter. Snuggle into it as it flows down through your hips, thighs, and knees. The darkness of tension and negativity is pushed further and further away. The beautiful light coats your lower legs, ankles, and feet like sweet, warm, honey, pouring energy, health, and positivity into them. Wash the last bits of negativity and tension out through your toes.

You are now completely and totally relaxed. All worries and tension are behind you. This is your time to focus on you. You are a sparkling ball of pure light, love, and energy. You are pure strength. Anything you wish to do is possible.

At this point it is time to do your visualization. It can be about anything. The one thing I will note is that in order for it to work, it must be about you. You can't visualize your way to a kinder older brother or nicer boss. Likewise, you can't use it to make someone like you. You can, however, use it to become a better diplomat in dealing with a brother, work on skills to find a new job and leave the rotten boss, or make yourself more likeable or have perfect timing to attract the right partner into your life.

Again, you need to tailor visualizations to whatever you want to accomplish in your life. I created a whole library of scenarios. Here's one of my favorite.

I see myself in my favorite spot—the beach. It's just before sunset. The sky is pink and orange with a few puffy golden clouds. The sun is a beautiful orange ball hanging low on the horizon. There's a gentle, warm breeze blowing. Above the crash of the waves, I can hear the distant call of seagulls.

I sit on the fine, white powder of the beach and roll my pant legs up. The sand is warm and soft beneath my feet. I pull myself up and begin to walk along the shoreline, smelling the salty air. I weave a trail from the dry powder of the beach down to the heavily packed wet sand at the water's edge.

I feel the moisture beneath my feet. The closer I walk to the sea, my feet start to sink a little, leaving deep impressions in the sand. When I pull my feet free, the sand makes sucking noises. I feel the slight pull on my feet and legs as the cement-like mixture tugs at me. A wave comes crashing in, sending water tickling over my feet.

Down the beach I see Ellen. I raise a hand in greeting and run toward her. I feel the in and out of my breath as my lungs expand and contract; I feel the impact of my feet hitting the sand, the way energy travels from my feet through my ankles up my legs and knees, through my thighs and pelvis, and the swing of my arms.

When I reach her, I grab her in a hug. Her blue eyes are incredibly intense. Her hair is as brilliant as ever. I smell her and feel the warm, softness of her body as we tumble to the ground.

In order for a visualization to work, make sure you incorporate as much detail as I did, until it feels so real, you could almost convince yourself you are there.

PHIL'S TOTAL BODY HEALING PLAN

When people ask for the exact formula I used to heal myself, I remind them that it was a total mind-body plan. I am not a medical doctor and I did work with and respect those who had a greater understanding of my particular medical situation. I simply supplemented their physical healing with a game plan of my own to balance the equation.

It wasn't a buffet to pick and choose from, I had to do all of it. Exercising just one or the other wouldn't have been enough because we are both mind and body. I offer my plan as a jumping off point and good foundation for others to build upon. Therefore, it's important to keep in mind that because everyone is different, it will be up to you to determine what is right for you and tailor your plan to fit your needs.

*Listened to the tape when I woke up for 30 minutes. The tape involved a combination of relaxation and visualization exercises.

*Exercised for an hour and a half using the plan I developed with my physical and occupational therapists.

*Followed my exercise routine with a set of affirmations. (Saw myself being able to walk now, in the present, not down the road.)

*Listened to the tape in the car on the way to work or to run errands. (30 minutes)

*Worked for 5-6 hours when I could.

*Listened to the tape in the car on the way home (30 minutes)

*Did another set of affirmations (These could be the same or different than the first set. No matter what I chose to say, I always saw myself as being able to have what I wanted, such walking freely and easily now, in the present.)

*Exercised, swimming for an hour and walking for 2 miles (45 minutes).

*Listened to the tape to practice relaxing and visualizing before going to bed. (30 minutes) This allowed me to imprint my desires on my mind, so that even in sleep my subconscious was working on them.

Overall I spent five hours a day working physically and mentally to reach my goals. I followed this plan full time for three years, seven days a week. Occasionally, I had to alter my plan to accommodate an appointment or family function. That didn't mean I took a day off. It meant I got up earlier to accomplish it, did a shortened variation of it, or replaced it with an equal activity/ exercise that would achieve the same results.

SUGGESTED INSPIRATIONAL READING

5 Steps to a Quantum Life by Natalie Reid

A Nickel's Worth of Hope by Andre Vandenberg

After the Darkest Hour by Kathleen Brehony, Ph.D.

Ask and It Is Given by Esther and Jerry Hicks

Awakening by Shakti Gawain

Being in Balance, (9 Principles) by Wayne Dyer

Creative Visualization by Shakti Gawain

Divine Magic by Doreen Virtue, Ph.D.

Feel the Fear and Do It Anyway by Susan Jeffers, Ph.D.

Going to Pieces Without Falling Apart, by Mark Epstein, M. D.

No Ordinary Moments by Dan Milman

Silent Power by Stuart Wilde

The Four Agreements by Don Miguel Ruiz

The Magician's Way by William Whitecloud

The Power of Now by Eckhart Tolle

The Vortex by Esther and Jerry Hicks

Think and Grow Rich by Napoleon Hill

CPSIA information can be obtained at www.ICGtesting.com
Printed in the USA
BVOW041839040413

317332BV00001B/16/P